# A SMALL AND

John Gibson was born spent two years sailing four-masted barque; he served as a submarine navigator during the war. He turned to writing in 1948 and worked also for a literary agency and Twentieth Century Fox's European Story Department. After ten years in Cornwall he emigrated to Canada and now lives in British Columbia. Mr. Gibson, who works for the Department of Social Welfare, has for many years been deeply interested in the history and culture of the Canadian Indians.

# A SMALL
# AND CHARMING
# WORLD

*John Frederic Gibson*

## A TOTEM BOOK
### TORONTO

First published, 1972, by Collins Publishers,
Toronto, Canada


This edition published 1976
Second printing 1976
by TOTEM BOOKS
a division of
Collins Publishers
100 Lesmill Road, Don Mills, Ontario


© 1972 by John Frederic Gibson

ISBN 0 00 211596 4

Printed in Canada by
Universal Printers Ltd. Winnipeg

# A SMALL AND CHARMING WORLD

# Contents

# *Preface*

THE world of which I write may be on the far side of a mountain; it can be on a Pacific island; it is across a lake; it is far away, or it is right across the street. If you have never known it, you might be surprised. If you have known it, you will remember. If you do not care, you might learn to care. Any world, however small, is filled with light and shadow, with tears and laughter. No book can do justice to the strength of the human spirit. No book is a substitute for life.

For many unrecorded years the Indians lived and died between Alaska and Cape Horn. The official history begins in the fifteenth century, and it is still being written. The reading of it is not always pleasant. In 1703, the colony of Massachusetts was paying the equivalent of about $75 for an Indian scalp. By 1827, there were no survivors of the once proud Beothuk of Newfoundland. The tribes of Terra del Fuego are extinct. In 1835, the Cherokee, who had achieved remarkable prosperity and sophistication, were forcibly marched a thousand miles to the west, over four thousand dying on the way. While this was happening, a report to Congress said: "The Government's handling of the Indian problem had been just and friendly, directed by the best feelings of humanity; its watchfulness in protecting them from individual frauds unremitting."

In 1968, the United Nations Conference of Human Rights investigated the massacre of Indians in Brazil. During the last decade, the Munducurus of Brazil have been reduced from 19,000 to 1,200; the Guarinis from 5,000 to 300; the Cintas Largas from 10,000 to 500. Many tribes are represented by a single family. This has been achieved by corruption, by the taking over of Indian land, the issue of clothing infected by smallpox, gifts of sugar laced with arsenic, by attack from the air. Within twenty years, we may see the complete disappearance of the native tribes of Brazil.

What has happened in the past is remote, separated by time. What is happening in the Matto Grosso is also remote, vague rumours from across the sea and from the depth of legendary jungles.

Closer to home, close to where I live and write, the native Indians of Canada are in their own villages or are scattered in the twentieth-century cities. They are known to politicians, to anthropologists and to those interested in primitive art. But, for the most part, the Indian is a shadowy figure. His image is rooted in the past, in the ageless myths of the frozen north, the pioneer and the bottles of fire water.

The truth is in the present. As with us all, the old men remember and the young men dream. There is also a day to be lived through, an hour, all the vital moments of time. Some of these moments have been brought together in this book.

# The North

*

# I

# Locale

NORTHERN BRITISH COLUMBIA has three main river systems, those of the Stikine, the Naas and the Skeena. The Queen Charlotte Islands lie off the coast. To the south, Vancouver Island shelters two hundred miles of tidal inlets which run into the uninhabited mountain country of the interior.

Most of the Indian villages are on the edge of the sea or on the banks of rivers. There are many different tribes and as many languages, but I am not concerned here with forgotten tribal wars or ethnic differences. The point is that the morning hours of a Haida child on her island home are much the same as those of a little Coast Salish girl on the mainland. The shadow of the totem pole will have a different outline, but the child will not be aware of it. She will have other things to worry about.

When, some years ago, my wife and I first drove north to the valley of the Skeena it was summer time; it was June. For almost a thousand miles, we moved into what was, for me, a very personal adventure. The adventure was to be on two planes. I was to fly and walk and drive and boat into isolated regions. I was to cross frozen lakes in winter time, to take my old car along mountain roads, to explore. On another plane, I was to uncover the thoughts and dreams and inner feelings of those who lived silently apart. In one way, it was to be an adventure of the heart.

The town in which we were to live for three years had been built on a swamp; it had a population of about three thousand. We rented a small, wooden house. Not far to the west, there was a circle of mountain peaks surrounding the green ice of a glacier. There were lakes and rivers.

My office was on the top floor of an ancient wooden building which had a coal furnace in the basement. The whole building smelled of hot wood and smoke as if it was about to catch fire. From the window, I sometimes saw moose wandering around in the snow and, in summer, the heat would burst out of the interior in a sudden wind which would bring down the fifty foot cottonwood trees. In spring time, when the snow melted, the side roads were yellow mud into which the wheels of the car sank to the level of the axles. In the surrounding hills and valleys, there were small mines and logging camps, sawmills and farms. There were no industries. The countryside was very beautiful, and we used to climb to the mountain peaks until we were between the clouds and the sky and heard only the sigh of the wind across the snow slopes.

From time to time, I visited the Indian villages in the Babine Agency.

## 2

# A Place called Moricetown

IT is called after Father Morice, one of the earliest and greatest of the Oblate missionaries. It sprawls along both sides of the highway, crosses the river and includes farmland, a lake, acres of forest. There must be two hundred people there, and you can find out about their tribe and language and culture by choosing the right book in the library. The highway is new, and you can drive past the reserve at seventy miles an hour if you so wish. Or you can make a forty-five degree turn to the right and drive into the main village and stop the car there. I took that particular turn one day and discovered a different world.

During the next year, I went through moments of despair,

depression, amusement, compassion, anger, humility and understanding. Writing about women, Freud said: Dear God. What do they want? Thinking about the Indians of Moricetown, I asked the same question: Dear God. What do they want? What did anybody want? The Indian Superintendent talked about self-determination for the Indian people. But self-determination did not mean that men could write to their Member of Parliament in Ottawa. There were limits. Everyone talked about integration, yet Indians were not served in local restaurants. The priest thought that the people wanted religion. The bootleggers thought the people wanted liquor.

A sanitary inspector arrived with a projector to show slides about the use of latrines. He also brought with him a pedal organ and used to sing hymns and other resounding songs in the village hall. He discovered that the people of Moricetown called him Mr Organ and was obviously flattered. The Medical Health Officer decided to train a young person from each reserve in First Aid. The boy from Moricetown travelled by bus to a distant hospital to take the course. Unfortunately, because of a misunderstanding, he was admitted as a patient, put to bed for two weeks and then discharged, completely cured. An old man who received a blind pension went moose hunting in October. After desultory negotiations with the Department of Fisheries, the men of Moricetown agreed not to gaff any more salmon in the river if the Department could persuade black bear to stop fishing.

Ideas conceived in government offices fell, for the most part, on deaf ears and on stony ground. Whatever the people of Moricetown wanted, their wishes were ignored or simply misunderstood. Captain Cook had been puzzled by the fact that the Polynesians compared favourably with the brutal and corrupt societies of Europe. Rousseau praised men of nature. In our time, Lévi-Strauss has analysed the intellect of primitive man. American scientists have travelled south to learn from the Indians of Peru. Many peasant societies have been washed out of existence by the flood of facile and banal influences from cities. Yet the Indian has somehow managed to resist, to survive, to adapt. He has proved himself to have more courage and loyalty than his white neighbours. And yet, standing in the centre of Moricetown one day in late summer I faced only the forlorn shacks and the long, dry grass and the little children covered by flies and a young woman so drunk that she did not see me as she passed. Behind me in the car was a brief-case filled with reports from Ottawa, recommendations, plans, programmes, regulations, reminders, orders, restrictions, application forms, warnings, lists and suggestions. Paper made from a million trees moved from office to office. Perhaps I was intoxicated that day myself, made drunk by the background of white mountains and the clarity of the air and the pristine quality of the village scene and the feeling of discovery. A new world was very welcome after the somewhat drab characteristics of the little town in which I lived. At any rate, I was half blind and did not see the broken windows and the squalor and the less pleasant things I had read about or had been told about. I did not care about them either.

I might, then and there, have started a new Flat Earth Society, carried away by my own first impressions and convictions. As it turned out, the forty-five degree turn from the highway became a constant habit and it was like the entrance to life. In summer time, one sat in the open, serene under a blue sky and surrounded by wild flowers and all the less Arcadian vestiges of necessity, fish bones and moose bones and old traps and empty wine jugs and tin cans. In cold weather, when it could be forty degrees below zero outside, one sat close to an airtight stove or on the edge of a bed or on the floor. And, little by little, the questions were answered. What do they want, Dear God? To be left alone. To be left alone to be themselves. To do things in their own way. To prove that there are other ways of living in the twentieth century. To avoid the consumer's Paradise offered by white society. To avoid people who asked stupid questions.

It was not really surprising that the conversations were less and less about my world and more about the internal affairs of the reserve. We did not talk about the Federal or Provincial administrations or about the storekeepers in town or about the police or the magistrate. We did not discuss money or cars. Nothing was said about politics. Days spent at Moricetown were very similar to those blissful climbing or sailing holidays without newspapers or radio. For some reason I was shocked when I learned how little government personalities and programmes meant to the people of that northern valley. The shock wore off.

Most of the people who came to the village from nearby towns did so because they were paid to make the journey or hoped to make money afterwards. The Indian Superintendent arrived for meetings of the Band Council. The people treated him with respect but were convinced that he was closely controlled by his boss, a remote and nameless man of superior meanness. These feelings were further strengthened by the periodical appearances in court of officials of the Department who were charged with the misappropriation of funds. What these unfortunate men had done was to transfer certain sums from the welfare account to the housing account or sell some unwanted stores in order to buy non-return valves for the village water system. These crimes could not be ignored or the criminals go unpunished. The result was that most Superintendents acted with extreme caution if they were within ten years of retirement. Also, Council meetings tended to be dull affairs during which a few dollars from the village account were put aside for road improvement or new hoses for the fire truck. These meetings were usually held at night and took place in the community hall. The Superintendent and the Chief Councillor sat at a table while the other two or three members of the Council leaned against the wall or perched nearby on one of the benches used by the weekly cinema audience. A few of the villagers attended if they had nothing better to do. Meanwhile, the rest of the people would be whooping it up in one of the houses down the road.

One woman journalist visited Moricetown and wrote later that the people were dangerous, thereby missing one of the most important characteristics of the coastal tribes. The people have remained passive, even indifferent, in the face of personal and collective insults and humiliations for half a century.

I was paid to visit Moricetown, my salary being less than the Indian loggers made in a good month. My home, which I had rented in summer time, was only half insulated so that in cold weather we were frozen into the confinement of three rooms and existed in that way for six months of the year. My car was old and sent out at the back a cloud of bright blue smoke as it burned quart after quart of oil. What to do at Moricetown? My message was vague. My instructions were not specific. In fact, it was very difficult for me to find a moment of silence into which I might speak and be heard. If people around me were not talking, they were laughing. They laughed a great deal, often at those things which might have made me weep or, at any rate, might have made me thoughtful. I used to listen, of course, and came to appreciate the swift mental change which jerked the Indians on to the correct wave length to greet a white visitor. The loud and vibrant and heated and amused exchange of words would alter completely when they were faced with an official from town. The stranger, someone like myself with drab clothes and a pale face, possibly with an ulcerated stomach, would have his say and depart. The moment the door was closed, all the old arguments would start, and memory of the visitor would be extinguished.

There was something very heartening about this indifference to authority, but it did not have a very good effect on my self-esteem. Other outsiders suffered. Just when the priest thought that he had a loyal and regular congregation, no one would turn up at the church on a Sunday morning. A senior member of the Department of Health and Welfare

arrived to give a lecture on the fact that cleanliness was next
to godliness. He prefaced the evening by asking for a
blackboard and drew on it a kind of family tree of his
administrative pyramid. His own name and position were
underlined in red chalk. In fact his name occurred very
frequently, like the tracer every sixth round. At the end of
the speech, one of the Indians turned to me and asked: "Who
exactly is that fellow up there?"

An official called Smith might serve the Indians in the
area for five years, working with diligence and fervour. For
five years, letters would arrive from the reserves. Dear Mr
Smith. Dear Smith. Hundreds of letters would come in each
month. Mr Smith might feel that his work and service were
recognised and appreciated. He had frequently placed his
middle-aged head on the Federal chopping block in order to
help one of the men in the agency. In due course, he would
be transferred. Transfers took place every three or four years
in order that the staff did not become too knowledgeable or
too sympathetic. Mr Smith would be followed by Mr Jones,
and from that exact moment all letters would start: Dear
Mr Jones, or Dear Jones. Poor Mr Smith's five years of duty
would be forgotten along with last year's spring flowers and
the winter snow and the dog which was run over by a school
bus on Highway 16.

"The Indians," said the wise man, "sit in apathy and squalor
on reserves instead of joining in the main stream of Canadian
life." I could have wished that he was right. I could have
prayed that the people stopped being so busy just for one
minute or one hour or one week of my time and their time.
In order to survive, they had to earn money by working;
they had to hunt and fish, cut wood, argue with storekeepers
and officials, argue with car salesmen, battle with one
another, struggle endlessly with or against the surrounding
world in order to retain individuality as an Indian tribe.
People less strong would have surrendered; they would have
become an amorphous mass of poorly paid loggers, living in

rented houses on the edge of the town and watching ethnic murder as their children were absorbed into the educational machine. Perhaps, if I had been given the opportunity to speak, my message would have been about integration and the main stream. As it turned out, I simply asked: What do you want? The answers kept me busy for three years. And each person had a different answer. Individual desires were simple, their complication being that they often appeared to make contradictions in families, in the band, in the tribe. Each person emerged from the mist and myth and irrelevance of race and colour. Those things I had thought would matter did not matter at all. And one day, looking up from a page of notes on which I had been concentrating, I happened to see my reflection in the glass of a window which framed the night sky, and I was different. My skin was white.

Dear God. What do they want?

Johnny wanted to know if it was all right to shoot one of the horses which had been hit by a truck. The horse lay on the edge of the highway. Its owner was away in the hills, looking for mountain goat. No one wanted to shoot the horse without the owner's permission.

Ernest wanted the logging industry to stop working over his trapline thereby ruining his income. He asked me to write a letter to his Member of Parliament about this and about the amount of compensation he should receive.

Esther wanted me to speak to her daughter, Rachel, who sat around all day and stayed out all night and who never helped with the small children or the cooking or the washing. Rachel wanted her mother, who had high blood pressure, to go to hospital and stop worrying about the small children and the cooking and the washing.

Helen wanted me to go over to Arthur's house and ask if she could have her baby back. Arthur had taken the child when Helen was in town to do some shopping and he refused to negotiate. Arthur wanted me to instruct Helen in the responsibilities of motherhood which included staying at home and not leaving the baby with a half blind grand-mother.

Peter wanted Tom to stop handing out free bottles of beer to people leaving the village hall after a meeting of Alcoholics Anonymous.

Charles wanted back four of his children who had been removed by order of the judge of the Family Court. The judge had decided, quite rightly, that one room, ten by twelve feet, was not enough of a home for eight people. Charles had applied to the Department of Indian Affairs for some lumber with which he might enlarge his house and had been told that since he now only had two children at home, he did not need the lumber.

Zelda, who came from one of the Tsimshian villages, wanted to know if it would be advisable for her to marry a Moricetown man.

George, who was in gaol, wanted freedom. He had been charged with assault after he had struck a white man who was threatening him with a rifle. George had taken the rifle away from the man in front of four witnesses. He had pleaded guilty.

Harry wanted some cows.

Marka wanted her husband to stop fooling around with Violet.

James wanted me to get out of his life and never come back. His wish was granted.

My memories of Moricetown are pleasant, for the days there were filled with gaiety and the sort of honesty that makes everything else unimportant. I hope there is no change. Sooner or later, someone will decide that a smelter will bring employment to the area and the expectation of life will increase. Infant mortality will decrease. The children will be better educated. But this will not be a complete solution, not quite. The loss will be in the intangible qualities of life, in independence, courage, fulfilment and purpose. Our form of progress will destroy something few of us have had a chance to know. The children who now survive, but who would once have died, will be the statistics of optimism; they will never know the price we have demanded or the manner of payment. And so they will be content.

## 3

## The Old Man's Family

THE car moves slowly over the unmarked whiteness of the road, and snow falls. It is a cold day in early winter, and the rivers still run; they are not frozen. The features of the landscape have not been covered and distorted by blizzards and drifts. It is strange how quickly one forgets the summer with the blue lake water and the wild flowers growing in meadows. One adapts like a ptarmigan.

Five miles from town a figure stands like a frozen sentinel at the roadside, and I slow down, recognising the old man who raises his stick. It is not easy to stop. If you apply the brakes quickly the wheels stop turning but the car continues to move forward and the sound is like that of a hand brushing silk. Eventually, I open the door and look back and see the figure limping along with his head down. Then he looks up and grins.

"Good. I thought I'd have to walk all the way. Twenty-five miles, eh?"

"Get in."

He heaves himself into the seat beside me. His right leg, which he once showed me, is a thing of twisted bone and bits of iron. It has been like that for a long time. But he moves around the country, picking up his pension cheque at the post office. He has no special address, and I find him sleeping on the floor of houses from one end of the valley to the other.

He must be eighty. He has an old, cruel face. His voice rasps as he tells me what life was like in the old days. When he was a little boy of eight, two white men came up from the south with pack horses. He said he could remember them clearly and his father had wanted to kill them but his mother suggested that they wait to find out what the strangers would do. The Indians watched but gave no help. The two white men, who wanted to start farming in the valley, found a cave in the hillside where they spent the winter. The horses died or were killed. And in the spring the ground around the cave was covered with porcupine quills. In the end, the Indians showed the strangers where the land was good and taught them how to live in the forest of the north.

The old man gives the impression of great strength; he has a large body of bone and sinew. His eyes are like green ice; they do not appear to see but move in the brown and wrinkled skin of his face, reflecting the snow. He does not look at me. He often appears to be deaf, ignoring my remarks completely. But his brain records what I say, and he may bring out one of my casual statements in a year's time, long after I have forgotten the day and the time of our meeting.

We move towards the north at a steady thirty miles an hour, a speed which I have found suits my car on snow and ice. I drive with one foot on the brake pedal and one on the accelerator, braking against the engine to avoid too sudden a change in momentum.

All this mechanical movement may be impressive, but the old man takes it for granted, and I do not feel in any way superior. In fact, he is probably thinking that he knew the valley before there were roads and telephones and cars and electricity. He may even know that I would have starved had I been there when he was a small boy. I certainly would have starved without his help. If the car breaks down, he will expect me to fix it and if I am defeated by the car I will earn his contempt.

Thus, the older Indians preserve a certain arrogance; they remember the time when they outnumbered the white man, had more knowledge of the locality and survived from season to season if they were careful. They remember winters when game was scarce and people died; they can look back on the days when the forest spread without a break from the Arctic watershed to the Pacific and travel was by trail or by boat. It is very obvious that I do not impress the man at my side. I am comparatively young, white, some kind of an official. I have come and I will go. The impact is insignificant. The old man has emerged from the past; he has outgrown even the joys of drink and lust. The great, macerated body serves to support a brain which is removed from the Stone Age by a generation. He is not of a post-Roman culture, and his main reason for living is to avoid dying. In his own lifetime, perhaps, his tribe has advanced along the path of evolution, forming within itself all the intricate patterns of the extended family, taboos and superstitions and rituals. He has witnessed changes in his own primitive society and then, subsequently, the gradual extension of Western civilisation across his little world. He is a Catholic. He has never been to school. He speaks his own language, but the Indian words were never written. He has known incest and murder. Now, he lives with his third or fourth wife. The only things that have not changed for him are the colours of the hills and the times of the salmon run, the seasons, the sounds of laughing children and the inevitability of death.

I look down at his hands. They rest in his lap, relaxed skin and bone, suitable as appendages of his gaunt frame. They are not clenched, nor do they move with the restlessness of the ulcerated business man who is so successful in the new world. The hands betray an indifference to me, to my race, to the things I represent. It is the same with the eyes. They almost exclude me from the foreground like a camera set only to record the broad aspects of distance. Not being concerned with the future, he can afford to dismiss me as a temporary phenomenon, a migrant bird of unknown species pausing briefly on its way to another clime. He is an oriental, fatalistic in some ways, a human bridge between the past and the future. And the thing holding him together is the valley, the land of his ancestors. He has the classic wisdom of the nomad. Every lake and river and valley and mountain within a hundred miles is known and used. Such knowledge was all that stood between his tribe and total extinction.

He does not talk much. His English is laborious. He can communicate well and in many different ways, but communication is not necessary at all times. Thus, as we sit in the warm car and look ahead through the falling snow, we are often far apart. He does not set out to tell me how wonderful life was before the white man took the land; he keeps away from all the myths, knowing that I know how hard his life has been and how inhospitable was the country into which he was born. He has no wish to return to the old days and sometimes complains that his pension is too small. But, for most of the time, we sit with our separate memories and dreams.

I ask about his family. He nods his head and laughs at a secret joke.

I ask: "What are you laughing at?"

"My family? I don't ask you about your family. Why ask me?"

"Where are you going today?"

"Just down the road. I tell you when to stop."

The old man does not worry when we move along the edge of a canyon with nothing between us and the hundred foot drop to the river. He is warm and comfortable. Sixty years ago he must have walked along the banks of the river in sub zero temperatures with nothing at the end of his journey but a turf hut and a piece of rancid fish. Now, he looks half asleep, but his mind is considering my words.

"You know my family? You know my wife?"

"Yes."

"Not my wife. My woman, eh?"

"Yes."

"You got a woman?"

"Yes," I say. "But not a large family."

It is a grey, sepulchral day, but the snow has stopped. We come to a group of small cabins, and the old man turns his head as if to see if there are any enemies in the shadows at the edge of the road. I stop the car. He thanks me and heaves himself out into the cold air. I watch him limping on his way, a rather sombre and lonely figure who cannot write a word but knows things I will never know and has memories few men share.

Not far away lives the old man's son, a morose character who works in logging camps when the opportunity arises. I drive for five miles and come to a wooden house which stands above the road and in a circle of trees. Three dogs lie under the house, and the snow is churned up by boots and firewood and animals and miscellaneous rubbish thrown from the front door into the winter day. I have never been in the house and approach it with some misgiving. The place is cheerless. Probably, the dogs will come out and bite the backs of my legs. Perhaps my car will not start again. I should have driven on to some more congenial destination.

After I have knocked on the door there is a subdued banging and shuffling of feet and then, while I grow cold, someone turns the handle and looks out at me through a four inch gap of darkness.

"Hello. Can I come in?"

The door opens, inch by inch. The man stands back, reluctantly, and I can see the red glow of a wood stove. It is too dark to read in the room, and I wonder what everyone was doing before I hit my knuckles on the door. The man nods:

"Sit down."

They have placed a chair by the kitchen table, a solitary chair on which I am expected to sit while the rest of the family stare out of the shadows. They are in a row, presumably sitting on a bed, and I can make out a woman, a girl of about sixteen, an older boy and four or five smaller children. There is nothing else in the room. One table, one chair and an iron bed. There are no pictures on the walls, not even a calendar. There are no toys. There are no newspapers or magazines.

There is no need to say anything for a few minutes. I am aware that the woman is muttering under her breath. The man stands against the wall. I am abruptly ashamed of my presence there, an obnoxious intrusion into the secret and hidden world of a family. I know that the man's name is Amos and that he has a reputation for being cruel, sour and friendless. His wife is bent and battered, unable or unwilling to speak English. But I know that she has great courage. Not long ago, and after a serious operation, she discharged herself from hospital and walked nine miles in the snow because she was worried about the children. What she does for the children when she is at home is not immediately apparent, but whatever it is she does it in her own way. I cannot judge her as a mother, because I do not know what she wants for herself or her children. She may not want anything; she may be content.

I am there because a letter has been written to me by the sixteen year old girl. She has sent a stilted note, pencilled words of extreme politeness. I sit on the hard chair in half darkness, and my presence there is an answer to her letter. She may want to leave home, because the oldest girl in some families is virtually a slave; she cooks and cleans and fetches water, tends the babies if there are any, mends clothes and brings in logs for the stove. When she has time she goes to school. Away from home, she becomes conscious of the class distinctions of reserve life. Another girl may have parents who are interested in education, in the white man's world. Other girls will have time to do homework; they will go to town and buy clothes; they are the bright ones on whom attention is concentrated.

The family in whose house I sit has not broken through the psychological barrier between the past and the future. It is not a matter of being more or less Indian, but the parents have at no time been able to move away from the condition of life governed by the acquisition of necessities. It is probable that all the children share one bed. The day is used up in the gathering of wood for warmth and food for survival. Very little of the outside world seeps through the intense concentration on hunger, cold and weariness. The old man's family has been frozen in an archaic situation which we like to describe with simple and inadequate words like poverty or deprivation or backwardness.

Because no family is the same and because individuals are all different, one from the other, reserve life is very difficult to describe. Each family has reacted in a different way to the presence of white society. The old man is perfectly content to die without learning to write. His son, Amos, went to the Indian school for a few years but he has never become deeply involved in the business of earning money and relating to people like the priest and the teachers and the civil servants. Amos is probably about forty; he has inherited or acquired his father's conceit and arrogance. But he cannot disengage from the facts of modern life. He has no pension. If he does not work, he is at the mercy of the current Indian Superintendent. His children are forced to remain at school until they are sixteen. The century of progress creeps like a fungus into the reserve, and Amos is a man who clings to tradition and refuses to listen. Year by year, he withdraws into the world of his father.

It is very easy for me to sit in that cold and cheerless room and have sympathy for the girl who might, for all I know, have ambitions to be a doctor or might be suffering from a tragic neglect of her emotions. There is nothing simple about the family, neither in the tension by which it is held together, nor the individual frustrations which will cause it to break apart. The girl, Donna, does not look at me, but I know what she feels. Today, she is a part of the family unit, a servant both to her mother and her grandmother. She is a bridge between the psychology of her father and that of her little brothers and sisters. What she does there is done because it has always been done. And when she has finished her work in the house she is free to live her own life, to visit friends, drink, make love, sleep. She is free to die.

She and I are both caught in a trap of time and circumstance. What can I say? Is it better to let her work out her own personal destiny without my intrusion? What right have I to be there? She is supposed to follow the example of her parents, to do her duty, to fit into the taut family structure without verbal advice, instruction or guidance. If I take her away, two things will happen. The family will become disorganised and bitter. She, herself, will for ever be excluded from reserve life; she will visit home as a stranger. But no one will prevent her departure.

Donna's father probably knows why I am there. He keeps the conversation going, but our words are almost meaningless. In the end, I stand up and shake hands and move with relief into the falling snow. The car starts and the heater is efficient and the radio picks up music from somewhere. And as I drive down the white road, I wonder what childish and innocent things Donna and her little brothers and sisters find to do.

She writes several times during the winter. Some of her friends bring messages or tell me about her life at home. I make oblique remarks about her to the old man, her grandfather, but he will not be drawn into any discussion about his relatives. Sometimes I feel that Donna is not on this planet but has appeared in a dream or in a novel by a dead author. Children normally have an existence outside their homes; they might be seen at school or in church; they are taken to a show by one of the boys. They are often solitary but are seen as they trudge on the roadside in sunshine, rain or snow. But Donna lives within four walls. She is the unknown girl who writes little notes with a blunt pencil.

I call at the house one day in late spring when the snow is still on the mountains but wild flowers colour the valley meadows and the green of the year is rising like coloured smoke beside the river.

There is little sign of life around the house, but I stop the car and lean on the wheel. The best way to appreciate spring is to spend winter in a place where the only natural colour is the green-black of the pines and where snow lies deep over the land. The sky can be a vivid blue in winter time, but the colours of spring are always breathtaking. Sounds change. It is possible to hear the river. The wind rustles in a million new leaves. One feels good. Perhaps it is the right day to call on Donna.

I walk up to the door, ignored by the dogs. A long line of children's clothes hangs out in the sun like a ship's signal. All the rubbish of winter has been left by the melting snow, bottles, orange peel, bits of metal, bits of wood, moose bones and a tattered hide.

Donna opens the door. She stands very still in the splash of sunlight, a slender figure in spite of her ill-fitting clothes. Then she steps outside and looks across the valley. I ask a question, and she turns away, head bent, leaving for me the silhouette of her face. She answers me with a slight opening of her lips. No sound. I can talk quietly about her friends, make inconsequential remarks, try to attract her attention. Her eyes are hidden. Her face is expressionless.

"You wrote me about leaving home. Do you still want to leave?"

The girl's lips move and there is a faint whisper. She seems to be poised as if expecting an attack. I can stare at the curve of her cheek and the black hair falling across her shoulders. I can stare without being rude. I remember that she is the old man's granddaughter and is the third generation, so to speak. As a result of the town and the road and cars and school and people like myself she is without confidence and the ability to communicate. She has, for some reason, remained in the world of the past. She has her duties, her role in the family and the abusive friction of drifting along the edge of the new century.

What can one promise? Perhaps her friends make fun of her. Do we gain a single centimetre by taking her from the familiar world of her unhappiness and dropping her like a scientist's specimen into the crudity of white society?

"Look at me, Donna."

She turns her head and observes me with dark eyes.

"Would your mother allow you to leave home?"

"I don't know."

"Shall I ask her?"

"Yes."

But she does not mean what she says. Her answers are a combination of politeness and impatience. It is difficult for her to think as I think, and her mind is restricted to the immediate present. I am not able to read much in her eyes which reveal only her innate distrust of strangers. Whatever I may say, Donna remains within her world; she is a very human part of that world. Her experiences have helped to form her character in a negative sort of way. Work is accepted. Sex is forgotten between dreary incidents. Love is unknown. Her thoughts have concentrated on hunger, day and night, heat and cold, loneliness. Each day is a self-contained lifetime. Obviously, she wishes that I would go away. My conversation is comparatively abstract. It is one thing to sit down and write a letter to a distant official but something quite different to talk with a man who arrives unannounced in a black and yellow car.

She turns away again, her head bent so that she can see only the wooden step and a part of the house wall. A dull view, but one more comforting and familiar than my white and angular face. I could talk to her about the Protection of Children Act or the Juvenile Delinquents Act or foster homes and group homes and receiving homes. I could extract her like a tooth from the family situation, but wherever she went she would be thought of as an Indian and saddled with the false image, the stereotype.

"Is that your dog?"

She raises her head. "Yes."

"What is her name?"

"Pootsy."

"Pootsy?"

Donna jerks her head and turns towards me as if annoyed, wondering if I am laughing at her.

I ask: "Do you have a cat?"

"Yes."

"What's the Indian word for a cat?"

"Puss."

"Is that an Indian word?"

"Yes. I don't know."

"What do you call the cat?"

She starts to laugh. "Puss. We call him puss."

"You like animals?"

"Yes."

"Would you miss the animals if you left home?"

The shadow returns to her face. I can see her lips move and hear the sibilant whisper. We are back where we started.

During the heat of the summer the land is very green except where white dust flies up from gravel roads. In Donna's village, the dogs lie and pant in the shade. The rivers look cool and liquid and inviting. In half darkness, beneath the forest trees, there is a luxuriant growth of ferns and moss and wild currants. But out in the open the grass is yellow.

I have not seen Donna for several months. Her brother waits for me one day, a slim and taciturn young man who looks like a Chinese army recruit, wearing olive green clothes and a cap of the same colour. He leans on the car and tells me that his mother is in hospital, his father working many miles from home and the children are without food. Donna is at home. The grandparents have been helping out but they are short of food as well.

We drive to the house, and the small children who have been playing outside dash for the door which they close behind them. I walk to the door and knock. This is an old routine, and it takes Donna a few minutes to let me in. Meanwhile, her older brother has wandered off towards where horses graze at the edge of the bush.

The inside of the house is stifling, and there is an acrid

smell of smoke and cooking fish. Donna and I go into the kitchen where a single pot sits on the stove.

"What's that?"

She peers at it. "Fish."

"Is that all you have?"

"Yes."

"No bread?"

"No."

"No milk?"

"No."

The boy comes in through the back door, and the little children come out from the bedroom where they have hidden themselves. Most of them wear shirts or vests but no pants. We stand in a rough circle and stare at the stove, and I notice that the water in which the fish floats is not boiling. Donna tells me that they have no more oil.

"Do you have an empty can?"

"No."

"A bottle, then."

The little children run through the back door and return with three wine bottles which they put on the table. I ask Donna to make out a list of food she needs and we all sit down on what chairs there are and on the bed or on the floor. There is a silence except for the scratching of the girl's pen. If I look through the window I can see the steeple of the village church and the pale, noon sky and the road where an old woman walks slowly in the heat. I am bemused by the fact that time passes so slowly and by the village atmosphere. My presence there is known to at least two hundred people, but I am not conscious of this; I am not given advice. I can feel the environment working away at my senses. Something happens to my awareness. It is like a tide of opaque water receding to reveal the clear and delineated picture of reality. In that hot and barren little home, I begin to appreciate something of life governed by the season of the year and the hour of the day. Now that she knows where the next meal comes from, Donna takes her time. It may be half an hour or an hour before the food is ready, and that period of time is simply an extension of the minutes when a person can be diverted. The tension of hunger and uncertainty vanishes. Donna even smiles at me as she presents her list.

We all climb into the car for the four mile drive to a store. On the way I consider the various foster homes which might accommodate the girl if she runs away from her family. Few would be suitable. Not many parents could slow down the process of integrating Donna into a fresh scene. The eager, busy, ambitious and middle-class people would fail simply because they sought success, because they assumed that Donna liked or admired them, wished to be like them, shared their competitive goals.

She and I go into the store, and I let her buy what she needs. Because she is a girl, she picks up a small jar of face cream. Because she is a child, she includes a comic book. And because she is kind, she chooses a box of chocolates for her mother in hospital. She is quick and efficient, moving around the store with her list in one hand. The storekeeper asks:

"Is someone going to pay for this?"

Donna does not answer. The man shrugs and comes over to me. "I had to cut off credit to this family. You know how it is."

"Send the bill to my office."

The girl and I carry the boxes to the car. It is pleasant to be in the day's heat and with the children again. The older boy, whose name is Peter, has been standing on a bridge, looking down at the river water. He strolls to the car, incurious and remote. Half way back to the village we realise that we have forgotten the oil. Everyone laughs. It does not matter. Someone will have enough oil to fill a wine bottle. In any case, Donna has bought some cold meat and cheese, and the house will be more comfortable if she does not have to cook.

I do not go into the house but sit in the car and watch the family, each person carrying something, wander up the path to the door. Only Donna looks back, and when I raise my arm in a farewell salute, she makes a small, self-conscious gesture with her right hand. It is not a gesture of gratitude but an acknowledgement of one person by another. For a moment, we exist in the same world.

She makes her move one day when the trees bend in a north wind and rain rattles on my office window. It is a day between summer and the first snow. She looks very small and forlorn, sitting on a hard chair with the water dripping from her clothes to the floor. In her own shy and unsophisticated way, she seeks my protection, and I am suddenly filled with despair. There is really no bridge between the two worlds, hers and mine. I am not able to refuse her request, but there is more disenchantment and sadness for her in the town than there would be among her own people. The change of environment will permit the free development of heredity. The old man was a strong, unfettered nomad. His son is confined on a reserve. His granddaughter has also been confined; she has grown up with her innate desires frustrated and warped. I can give her freedom from want, from abuse, from drudgery and squalor, but I cannot protect her from herself. Once free, she will be like a wild bird released from a cage.

On the far side of town, on the mountain slope, lives a cheerful Scandinavian family who cut their own firewood and keep cows and live off the land as much as possible. Donna and I drive over there and sit in the kitchen and discuss the future. We talk about clothes and health and school and responsibility and authority and behaviour. Donna looks out of the window; she is preoccupied with her own thoughts. Perhaps she thinks of the day when she goes home for a brief visit, dressed in her new clothes and carrying presents for her small brothers and sisters. She will be neither welcome nor unwelcome. She will be like a stranger, released from all the pressures and duties and hot-house tensions of village life.

When I leave she does not look at me.

In the morning, the Scandinavian foster mother telephones to say that everything is under control. Donna has had her baptism of washing and scrubbing and having lice removed from her hair. The doctor will probably find scabies or impetigo. The school teacher will discover that Donna is well-behaved and completely silent. She will sit alone, play alone and walk home alone. It is almost as if she denies the world around her. From time to time, she goes home to help her mother. She starts a strange and difficult life in two worlds, both of which are known to me.

Thus, as the first winter snow covers the trees with a grey mist, I sit in the house of Donna's grandmother and aunt and cousins. The old man lies on a bed in the corner, pretending to be asleep, because he cannot be bothered to talk. It is lunch time. There is a great deal of noise. Eight people sit around the table and eat, laugh, argue, shout. When I arrived, the noise stopped as if a radio had been turned off, but now it increases. Donna's aunt admonishes the small boys and girls who reach across the table for sugar or milk or jam. The older girls eat carefully and slowly, eyes downcast. A boy of eighteen leans back in his chair and grins; he has a black cowboy hat on his head. The grandmother is in command, and it is from her pension that the food has been bought. Any relative who is unlucky or out of work or ignored by the Indian Superintendent will come to the grandmother's house to eat. Someone hands me a plate of beaver meat which looks and tastes rather like the meat off a turkey's leg. And outside the snow falls.

The boys have cut and stacked wood in an old barn not far from the house. In their own rather casual way they have prepared for the short, cold days ahead; they have smoked and canned salmon, killed a moose, mended a couple of windows and bought, on credit, a drum of oil for the lamps. There is not much left to do. For a week, they are free. In their own house on their own land they can ignore the rest of the world and be themselves.

Even I can feel the protective and invisible wall around the village. It is the same wall that encloses the ghetto and the convent, a mute, psychological barrier beyond which the minority is safe, diversity is accepted and tension reduced. If Donna's aunt drives into town she will have to accept humiliation and discrimination, for she will not be permitted to rent a hotel room; she will not be served in the restaurants. A day in town is necessary once in a while, and after thirty years people are accustomed to attitudes and images. The stereotype Indian, either drunk or silent and withdrawn, has become a feature of the landscape and is supposed to be understood by experts.

It is very different in the old man's home. No one is drunk, and the noise is deafening. The girls who are picked up and dropped so casually by white men in beer parlours are modest and virginal. I feel at home, and everyone is polite. There is no sign of poverty or deprivation. The room is filled with its own unique and strong atmosphere, a distilled drop of historical experience and natural heredity. However, no one could call the village Arcadian. There are a great many feuds, arguments, jealousies and hatreds. The heat of personal feelings rise and die away quickly and without bitterness.

Nobody asks me about Donna. Peter, who is sitting in the corner of the room, observes me with his dark green eyes, a stare of indifference and slight contempt. He is not offered food, nor does he ask for it. He is uncomfortable, because the grandmother's charity embraces all children and grandchildren but has limitations. There are exceptions. Often, the young men hover on the fringe of the family group and suffer in silence as their pride and hunger compete. Donna's mother is not present; she would ignore me in any case. When I pass her in the village from time to time, she turns towards me a face that is like a flat and battered forehead with eyes, nose and mouth in appropriate places, and mutters some uncomplimentary obscenity. Or perhaps she is simply saying: "Good morning." Who knows?

Donna's aunt hands me a mug of hot coffee. I look out of the window, and the village is nothing but shadowed shapes of houses behind the snowflakes with figures moving back and forth like black and cretinous hunchbacks. One man pulls behind him a sledge stacked with firewood. He leans forward and exerts his strength against ropes which are around his shoulders.

When I turn my head I see that the old man has raised himself on one elbow and has fixed upon me his pale, unwinking stare. He grins like a dog and says something in his own language and everyone laughs.

"What does he say?" I ask Donna's aunt.

"He asked if you were going to put him in a foster home."

"Not yet. When he reaches his second childhood."

"He's still in his first," Donna's aunt says.

It is time to leave, but I do not look forward to a long drive in fresh snow. I am very reluctant to say goodbye to the happy and unsensational family which has so many attributes of strength and solidity in its own world and so few outside. The white man's acquired sense of superiority is as ruinous and overwhelming as a Panzer column. Beyond the privacy of their homes, the Indian people are obediently and sardonically inferior. Only the old man is immune; he has lived long enough to remember another day and another truth.

Donna's future unfolds with the slow and inevitable passing of the days. She has a peaceful year in the Scandinavian foster home; she has a few friends in town. When she makes a social call to the office, she talks without bending her head or turning her back. She returns to school where she studies what is known as domestic science. In spite of many things, she trusts people or she trusts them before learning to distrust them. A man gives her a ride down the highway, kicks her out into the spring rain and throws her suitcase into a water filled ditch. She is seduced and conceives, thereafter concentrating calmly on the business of making baby clothes. Her favourite saying is: "I'll be all right." She has her baby and turns out to be a careful and responsible mother. What is the end for me and the beginning for her is her marriage to a man ten years older than she is, a lonely derelict who is compassionate and grateful and kind. That is the main thing. Donna finds her place in the larger and less charming world of Western civilisation.

There are many things that create a climate for violence. It might be the summer heat trapped in the mountain valley. For a young man, it can be the frustration of being unemployed, without money, without much hope. It might be waking up each morning with an expectation of emptiness. What is there to do? Walk down to the store and try to charge a packet of cigarettes. Go across to the sawmill and hang around in case there is work to be done. Walk home. Wander across to grandmother's house and watch other people eating. Thumb a ride down to the office of the Indian Superintendent and sit in the hall for an hour so that a clerk can tell you to return in three days time. Try the Social Welfare office where the same wait is followed by the same answer. Wander down the street and look in the store windows. Pass the places where you cannot get served even if you have money. Thumb a ride home and sit in the silent house. Lie on a bed and stare at the roof for a while. Nothing to do. There is not even anything to think about. You end up hungry and hot and a little angry.

Peter goes through a long summer without work and he is often alone. He is in love with a girl who lives across the valley, but he rarely sees the girl because she is kept in the house to look after little children. She may come to a village dance. He might meet her in the store. But their relationship is shy and youthful. And so the days pass and the sun rises in a clear, white sky. Peter spends more time lying on his bed or sitting on the grass outside the door and throwing sticks for the dogs. If he works for a few days, he has to travel forty miles to a forestry camp and as soon as his pay cheque arrives, the storekeeper is there to take all but a few dollars. Donna comes to visit him and she lends him a little money.

One night, a Saturday night when there is a full moon, Peter hears that his girl has been attacked while returning home from visiting a friend. He climbs off his bed and walks down to the village. The place is distorted by moon shadows, and there is very little to see but the dark road and the small, square windows of the houses, light from the oil lamps dim through curtains. There are several men by the church, their cigarettes red and vivid under the stars. He hears a certain voice and recognises the silhouette of an older man. He has something to do at last, something to say. You do not need money to revenge the girl you love. You do not have to ask a white man what the next move should be. His anger is quiet now. He is almost serene. But the only response is a burst of laughter and a curse and a heavy boot in his stomach.

He goes away and finds a bottle. It is always possible to find a bottle in a house where a party has been held during the evening. In his own home, he drinks and broods and drinks again. Towards morning, when the pressures of the weeks and months and of the immediate humiliation, are pounding in his head, he takes down his father's rifle and runs towards the village. He feels strong, heroic. A few people call to him through the early sunlight. Someone shouts. A man stands in his path in an effort to prevent violence. Another figure appears. Now, the futile and endless and overwhelming frustrations build up inside him like the compression of all the hate in the world. He will no longer be stopped. He raises the rifle and fires, and a body lies on the road for an hour until the police arrive.

The old man sits beside me in the car once again. He grins as if he is glad to see me. After a while, I say that Donna seems happy. I was sorry to hear about Peter. The old man turns his head, but he does not speak; he stares out past my shoulder at the mountains on the far side of the valley, and his eyes are without compassion. He sees things in the landscape that I do not see; he remembers many things of love and death I do not remember; he feels things I do not feel. Perhaps he is thinking of all those who did not have the strength and endurance to survive as he has survived. It is so easy for me to feel sad about one young boy as I drive down the new, smooth highway. In a little while, I will be home in the world of optimism and progress. Only for a brief instant am I aware of the strength of human spirit emanating from the old man at my side. It is almost like a physical shock. I have rubbed shoulders with a warrior from the Assyrian hills.

## 4

# People of a Small Place

THE land around the head waters of the Skeena River was the last part of British Columbia to be opened up for white settlers. The Tsimshian Indians who lived along the coast had prevented white traders from travelling inland. Even when early missionaries and explorers arrived from the east, some villages remained apart. One of these was Kitwancool.

The village first appears in the census records in 1889 with a population of 195. As a result of tribal wars and disease, the number of people living at Kitwancool had dwindled, but the tribe had always been independent and autonomous. They had disliked interference, and, on one occasion, soldiers and police had been sent to the area to assist the local authorities. It was difficult for a white man to pass through Kitwancool as late as 1920.

The Gitksan people of Kitwancool fought long wars of attrition against the Tsetsaut, now extinct, in order to preserve their hunting grounds. Today, arguments persist over the ownership of land. The Indians of British Columbia had never signed a treaty with representatives of the British Government and they did not consider the Indian Act to be an interesting or binding document unless it was to their advantage.

There were two ways to Kitwancool. I used to drive down the south bank of the Skeena, pass the Kitseguecla reserve and then cross the river on a rather primitive car ferry which ran every two hours or when the crew felt like it. When the river was low, you had to cross thirty feet of beach and then drive up planks on to the raft. There was no engine. The raft moved along under a wire cable which was suspended across the river. A small wire went from the ferry and through a pulley on the cable and then back to the raft. The force of the river's flow on the rudder acted like wind on a sail. Sometimes, when the river was full and fast flowing, we would sag downstream and had to take in slack on the wire in order to hit the right place to land. If the river was sluggish, crew and passengers used long poles to help with the normal propulsion.

The ferry did not run in winter time when the river was frozen. It was one of the pleasures of summer, and I enjoyed leaning on the wooden rail and listening to the water and watching the Indian village of Kitwangar grow closer as the minutes passed. Seen from the bank, the Skeena was not an attractive river; it was usually yellow and opaque. But it was different from the ferry. You could see all the mountains upstream and the varied greens on the shore and the line of the Kitwangar totem poles on the north bank. It was quiet on the river, even refreshing after an eighty mile drive in the clear heat of the day.

After leaving the ferry, you passed through the old settlement which dated back to the days of the river boats and was sustained by the railway. Four miles to the north, the road divided. The right fork followed the river for thirty miles and was the winter road from Hazelton. The left fork went to Kitwancool; it was a new road, and it followed the twelve mile trail which had been the only way up to the village until recently. It was quite a good road. In some places it was built along the side of a hill with steep cliffs above and below. Moose or mule deer had to trot along in front of the car until they found a way into the trees. There were many black bears in the district, and sometimes I saw a fox or a lynx or a bobcat crossing the road.

The village lay in the centre of a wide valley, but it was a mountain village and it was almost unique because it was not beside one of the main rivers up which the salmon came. It had not been a summer camp for nomads nor a temporary settlement made permanent by the early missionaries. It was quite small. There were about fifteen houses. The road went through the village for three miles and then stopped at the edge of a lake.

I had first driven up there in a snow storm when all the young saplings bent down across the car and there were few indications of the road's exact position between the trees. On such a cold day, Kitwancool seemed bleak, only the sides of the houses visible through the screen of snowflakes. I had not returned until the summer, and the difference was extreme. The valley was green, the sky blue, and there were small clouds over the mountains. I drove to the home of the Chief Councillor to whom I made an explanation for my presence. This was a necessity, because I wanted to look at the lake and knew that some visitors had been trapped at the end of the road. The men of the village simply took out their power saws and dropped a few trees behind the cars. Once, a stranger had passed through the village to look at land to the north; he had considered ranching up there. The band council at Kitwancool wrote a formal complaint to the Premier of British Columbia. The farmer, meanwhile, emerged from the forest and said he would never return. Each night, and whenever he was away from his camp, one small part of his equipment vanished. He did not see or hear anyone. He only knew that he was watched wherever he went.

At a time when the Indian bands were invited to make their own bye-laws, a programme called self-determination, all the villages were asked to vote on whether or not liquor should be allowed on the reserves. Most of the bands in the area voted to have liquor. One or two of the more self-righteous bands voted against having liquor. The people of Kitwancool did not vote at all. They said that such matters could be handled without interference by the Federal agency. There was, in any case, no serious problem of drinking in the village.

The church at Kitwancool was like a miniature Notre Dame; it had two towers, and the minister was of the Pentecostal denomination; he came from the United States but lived fifty miles away in Hazelton. Originally, the people of Kitwancool had been Anglicans but they had changed their faith when the Anglican minister was late for a funeral. His car had skidded off the road on the edge of the Skeena River. So the Pentecostals moved in and were well received. There must have been something in their hellfire and damnation creed which appealed to the native soul.

On a summer afternoon, the village was almost deserted. A few families had already gone to the coast to prepare for the fishing season. Some of the men had climbed one of the hills to the west on a hunting expedition, and their wives were worried because nothing had been heard from them for three days. If the men killed a moose, they would light a fire, and a thin line of smoke coming from the trees would signify success in the hunt. Children were playing outside the school; they told me that the teacher was resting. He was a young man from London who had planned to write a book but had become lethargic in the atmosphere of the silent hills; he taught the small children when he was so inclined, ate a little, slept and disliked being disturbed during his siesta hour.

At the northern end of the village was a house in which one could buy chocolate bars and bottles of ginger ale. I used to go and sit in the kitchen and listen to voices on the two-way radio which was left on all the time so that it was a part of the day's entertainment. You heard the men from the Forest Service talking about what they would like for lunch and where their sandwiches could be left for them along the road. There were a lot of conversations between experts on logging or roadbuilding who talked their own jargon and hated to be interrupted by a woman who was trying to have a bag of flour sent up from the town.

Outside, the dogs slept in the shade, and humming birds darted through the trees. The old totem poles leaned above the graves. There was a superficial atmosphere of timelessness, but, in fact, the twenty-first century was rushing towards Kitwancool just as it was approaching Paris and London and New York. The village resembled those of the Carrier Indians to the east, but the resemblance was only visual and it was an accident of time. Kitwancool had been a permanent community with a developed society; it had possessed long houses, many finely carved poles, a strong culture, a history of success in war and all the customs and taboos of an advanced tribe. Kitwancool was gradually losing its strength, and the past would never be repeated. The Carriers, on the other hand, were from the interior; they had adapted to the search for game in a harsh land long before moose and deer were plentiful; they had lived by moving, and their homes had been skin shelters and turf huts. Their transition was towards a future of comfort. Their past was almost forgotten except by those who admired courage and fortitude.

Why should it surprise me when the Kitwancool people built their own community hall and had their own electricity plant before the government school was wired? Or that the men owned logging trucks and built their own houses without help from the Department? If these things betrayed an independent spirit, they also indicated that the old Indian life was doomed. Once the white man's technology was accepted, someone had to pay the bill. If a man from the village wanted steady employment he would have to work in the valley and he would need a car. He would need a telephone. Sooner or later he would grow tired of driving fifty miles to work and would take his family away from the mountains and the totem poles and the grave houses and the unspoiled country of white clouds and quiet people. Already, the older children were returning from school at Edmonton with new ideas and knowledge. But the small children still learned Indian from their grandparents. People who stayed in the village did not change. Progress meant the acquisition of technology; it had nothing to do with the loss of an inheritance.

When I stood on the northern edge of the village there was nothing between me and the Yukon border, four hundred miles to the north. There were no roads up there, only mountains and valleys, lakes and rivers and all the wild life which was eluding the hunters. Nearby, outside one of the old log houses, was a bright blue car which was owned by a girl whose name meant Little Raven and who could speak fluent French and discuss the arguments about Bacon and Shakespeare. In the house opposite, right across the road, the woman told me that she did not want water piped into the house. The correct place for water was outside.

Sometimes at Kitwancool I needed an interpreter and used to be helped by Peter Williams who was the village President and a chief of both the Frog and the Wolf clans. His Indian name was Gu-gul-gow. On the particular summer day when I talked to Little Raven about her blue car, Peter Williams led me to a white house in the middle of the village and asked me to sit down in the corner of the room. It was cool and dark inside. The two old people who lived there took very little notice of me. The woman had white hair; she had the beautiful, dark eyes and the long, tapered hands of a Parsee and she spoke very quietly, exchanging remarks in her own language with her husband. I remembered her daughter, tall and wearing a scarlet dress when she came to see if I could arrange to have her two children boarded while she was in the TB hospital in Prince Rupert.

Peter Williams told me that the grandparents of the children were worried; they wanted to know why no foster home in Kitwancool had been chosen. Why had the children been made wards of the government when there were so many relatives willing to care for them? Why had we not consulted the President? Could I explain?

It was difficult to justify my actions, because it was useless to quote the Act or the regulations or to use my authority or fall back on bureaucratic mumbo jumbo. I had to be convincing by the standards and customs of Kitwancool, and to do this I had to understand their village and class distinctions, their attitude towards one another.

I said that we took our instructions from the children's mother who had visited several foster homes and the home on the Hagwilget reserve. She had made all the decisions.

Why had the children not been sent to Kitwancool?

I explained that all foster parents were asked to have a chest X-ray, and I knew that the grandmother would not pass this test. It would not be right to send the children to any other home in the village. They might not stay there. They would probably return to the house they knew. Difficulties might arise.

My remarks were translated into the Tsimshian language, but the real communication was beginning to take place. The grandmother looked into my eyes, observed my hands, made me aware that she was willing to trust me if I so desired. This was always the critical moment, because you had to know what was taking place. You had to remain silent so that the person you were with received, so to speak, your acknowledgement. Had I, at that instant, continued to chatter about government policy, I would have failed, and my words would have been dismissed. To talk into such a silence, was like interrupting a vital statement. It was inexcusable.

By the summer day I was at Kitwancool, this pattern of

thinking was automatic. It was like thinking in a foreign language, but it was less useful when talking with younger Indians who had lived in cities for several years. In any case, by the time the grandmother and I had penetrated into one another's thoughts, she was asking what I was going to do with the children and not why I was doing it. I mentioned a family at another reserve, trying to pick someone who had the same social status, neither a coast Indian who had come inland nor a person of mixed blood nor a couple who had offended in some way. Perhaps the woman had married into her own crest or clan. Perhaps the husband had taken over a house which should have been left empty.

It was over an hour before we reached an agreement. I said that I would consult one or two families and write a letter if the children were accepted. When I walked out into the sunshine, the valley looked very beautiful. The carved poles stood against the blue of the hills. The Chief Councillor was sitting outside his house, a small man who spoke little unless he had something important to say. I remembered that his father had fought in the wars against the Tsetsauts and that his grandfather had been killed in one of the night attacks. It was strange that the New World was so close to ancient history. Overhead, there was a white trail across the sky as a jet bomber flew down from Alaska.

At Kitwancool the houses seemed to stand in haphazard disarray, and although there was now a road encircling the greater part of the village it was an afterthought. In fact, all the older villages and those where there were no cars formed a less organised pattern. If the village was on the water, the houses followed the beach. But the traditional picture was plainer at Kitwancool. The houses were farther apart; they must, at one time, have had a special place, a designed position where the family pole stood upright above the graveyard. However, only when the government started to build the box-like homes of this century was there anything like a street.

There were five Gitksan villages on the upper Skeena. They were all very different. In spite of intermarriage and visiting back and forth, the people were different. The pattern of life was similar, but Kitseguecla and Kitwangar and Kitwancool were not simply divisions of the same clan. Historical experience had set them apart, one from the other.

I often used to wonder about this. All the Indians I had met, whether from the coast or the interior, and all those I had read about, from Alaska to Cape Horn, had a common heritage and a similar outlook on life. They retained an individuality and a strength of purpose which could only have been passed down to them by heredity. What they had learned from white men was usually demoralising.

The subtle differences between village and village or between man and man must have come from the environment. The society of the Gitksans had been complex. Chiefs' sons could only marry chiefs' daughters. Commoners did not marry slaves from other tribes. The abandonment of customs and rituals had depended on the strength of purpose and influence of the first missionaries. The transition was uneven. First impressions were very misleading. One might assume that the people of a village which was isolated would be closer to their own culture. This was not always the case. Nor was it true that technical progress and prosperity led to sympathy with and imitation of the white man. The people of Kitwancool were progressive but had no great desire to integrate. The men and women of Kitseguecla lived near the railway and the highway but they remained in their own shadowed world where the dark spirits of the hills still intruded on human relationships.

Luckily for me, perhaps, I was always talking to an individual, and, after a while, the intricate and distasteful questions of race and colour and religion and tribe evaporated with the morning dew. I could afford to pity the preachers or the Indian Superintendents or the politicians who were caught in a sticky web of unfulfilled expectations. Very few of the plans conceived in the committee rooms of

Ottawa penetrated to the minds or hearts of an individual native Indian.

If I wanted to see one of the Kitwancool men during the fishing season, I drove two hundred and fifty miles to Prince Rupert. I would be lucky if I found the man, but it was possible to observe the answer to the question: How does the salmon get into the can?

Each summer, Pacific salmon in their millions leave the centre of the ocean and head for the rivers of the west coast. They are met, some miles off shore, by an immense fleet of white fishing boats, the seiners first, with the small gill-netters in the shallow water near the river mouth. The docks near the old town, the inlets, bays, estuaries and coves were filled with the boats, their masts sticking up against them like a forest of dead trees. The Indian boats tied up near the cannery; they went to sea at dawn, fished for a while and then returned with their catch. The fish were thrown into bins and subsequently arrived in the building where a bloody and strong smelling system of perpetual motion began. Each fish advanced on a moving board, and its head was neatly guillotined by a blade which went up and down at a regular but unspecified interval. Eventually, what was left of the fish was edible. This went into a vat and was cooked.

The men brought their families to the coast, and the people lived in small, square cabins which had been built above the tidal mud flats and were joined by old wooden catwalks. Most of the wives and older daughters worked in the cannery, standing in lines as the cans came past and dropping in the required amount of pre-cooked fish. Thus, for a few months, all adult members of the family had an income. This was probably a relief for the men; it was a godsend for the women who were able to walk into the town in the evenings and go to the cinema or drop into the beer parlour or buy clothes and cosmetics.

Not long ago, a visiting journalist wandered into the cannery area and later wrote a vitriolic article about the conditions in which the Indians lived, the danger of children playing above the high tide, the slave labour, the lack of sanitation, the number of people crowded into one small room. In the interests of his own standards and way of life, he would have stopped the summer customs of the people from the mountain valleys. He may not have realised that when they were not in Prince Rupert the people were dependent on inconstant employment in logging camps or on reluctant assistance from the Federal Government. What he said was perfectly true, of course, but if any of the Indians read his article they would have been amused and startled. After all, they had electric light and television and piped water. They had work. The old people made nets and the young people canned fish and the men were out on the sea. It was all very much like a holiday.

The economics of the fishing was simple. Men rented boats for five hundred dollars and nets for three hundred dollars. They could charge all the food they needed in the company store. At the end of the season, they either ended up with a cheque or owed the company money, depending on the size of the catch. Debts were carried over to the following year. Money made by the women was not included in the fishing account and was paid every two weeks at an hourly rate. On the whole, everyone profited. The system was as fair as any other commercial enterprise, and those men who owned their boats and nets were often plagued with expenses which reduced some of the pleasure and pride of ownership.

At the end of the season, successful fishermen returned to their villages, their cars filled with television sets, furniture, cameras and all the impedimenta of the world of success. Those who had caught only a few fish returned empty handed. But next year would be better. It was very important to remember that a poor season was followed by a good season. That particular rule applied every year. It was something to think about during the long, cold winters of Kitwancool.

# 5

# Small Talk at Hagwilget

U P behind Hagwilget wild orchids grow in the long, summer grass, Lady Slipper and Cyprepedium. A bird, it looks like an osprey, glides across the face of the mountain. The Indian village is just east of the high level suspension bridge across the Skeena River. The width of the valley at that point is meadow and grassland, not many trees. In the southern background is the peak of Rocher de Boule, and the highway passes three miles to the south.

Hagwilget is not isolated, but it does not attract tourists. There are two totem poles. The village is simple, almost absurd in its conformity to certain artistic principles. For instance, the aspect presented to passing motorists is of small houses encircling a hill on which stands the church so that the spire rises far above the community. But Hagwilget is important for two reasons. It is the farthest westward point of the Carrier Indian approach to the coast, and it is the only Catholic reserve in the area.

Perhaps because it was so easy to reach, I often drove past Hagwilget without stopping, and yet my memories of that place are always pleasant. The people were full of charm; they combined a dry humour with a philosophical detachment from their surroundings. Even the local priest, who was something of a theological scholar, was defeated by the equanimity of the people there. Christian virtues, like forbearance and unselfishness, led to a disregard of man-made rules and moralities. Equally, many of the people ignored the paternalism of the Federal Government which meant that the agents were unable to use their sticks and carrots of manipulation.

I enjoyed visiting the chief who was an old man. He lived

in a dark brown house which he had built himself. He looked like a cross between Robert Louis Stevenson and Trotsky, and spent many hours of the week in bed. I would sit by the bed, and he would tell me about the old days when he had worked on the construction of the bridge and had been a reserve policeman. His children and grandchildren were sometimes allowed in the room and on special occasions were given permission to sit down.

Philip was an autocrat; he governed in the Indian way which was by example. He did not rule. In another house, there was an elected chief, a sort of mayor who was responsible to the representative of the Federal government for reserve planning. At that point, the pretence at democracy came to an end. The Superintendent of the agency could veto most of the decisions of the band council, or, if he did not do so, someone in Ottawa did. The elected chief was a symbol. The old man with whom I talked was the hereditary chief and he had much influence in the village.

In summer time we would sit out in the sun near the vegetable garden which was carefully cultivated by the women. The old man had several married sons and daughters and many more grandchildren. The family spread out into five houses in the little community, but Philip's house was the largest; it was a refuge, not only for grandchildren, but also for uncles and aunts and cousins who came to visit from other parts of the Province. No one was ever refused a bed or a meal. This traditional pattern was unintentionally preserved and strengthened by Federal and Provincial legislation. At a time when old age pensions were seventy-five dollars a month, a widow with two children living on the reserve received only thirty-nine dollars a month from the welfare account. Thus, grandparents were always wealthy, and the structure of the extended family survived.

Philip liked to talk to me about his relatives, and he would often ask for help in his struggles on behalf of the weak or the misguided. He was critical of those who drank too much, but would never side with the police or the Indian Superintendent against his own people. He had witnessed the slow and terrible disintegration of the native culture and he knew, far better than I, how deep was the humiliation. I could not share his memories, but it was obvious that the early missionaries and Government agents had used his influence. Now, they chose to disregard him unless he agreed with current policy. All this he accepted with a shrug and a smile.

Philip's house was always filled with children. Beds were made up in all the rooms and in the passages between rooms. At meal times, there were often ten people around the table. When there was unemployment in the area, food was short, and many men would prefer to send their children to eat at Philip's than beg for money from the Government agent. It was a question of pride. One man refused to visit the Agency office and eventually left the reserve and lived with his wife and eight children in a two-room cabin on the far side of the river. I used to visit him there. He was quite content. Small black bears used to follow the children down the trail to the stream where the family collected their water.

When he was feeling old and sick, I would sit by Philip's bed and we would discuss the young people of the village. He had not abandoned his principles where children were concerned and still believed that one did not interfere with young people nor explicitly instruct them in day to day activities. He also knew that times were changing and that the influence of the white man was predominant. So he would use me, asking me to talk to Joan or Mary or George or Charlie. He asked if I could stop the white boys coming on the reserve on a Saturday night with whisky and beer and empty seats in the car for any girl who felt like a night drive. He wanted someone to intervene when a bulldozer belonging to the Department of Highways went through the Indian graveyard and left a collection of bones and skulls scattered on the dry ground. He worried about the school. He knew the importance of education.

We did not really solve the problem of the graveyard.

Probably our complaints were a nuisance to some distant official who had never heard of Hagwilget and was only interested in widening the road during the summer months. But for a few weeks the tension was great. The Indians were asked to move the remaining graves and the Department of Highways would pay the costs of reburial. Meanwhile, we discovered that there were bones enough for six bodies but only four skulls. The earth had been removed and had already been used to make an extension of the playground in the parochial school. It looked as if the skulls were now embedded somewhere in the playground. The priest thought that maybe he could solve the whole problem by blessing the football field. And, shortly afterwards, the Department of Highways sent up a wooden box which was supposed to be used for storage of any other bones upturned by the yellow bulldozer.

Philip was not satisfied by all the token apologies and solutions offered by the authorities. His carefully worded and polite letters must have exasperated the officials in Victoria whose only way of judging right and wrong was to assess the amount the bulldozer was costing the taxpayer while not in use. The game continued, but it was one which had to be played with extreme caution. The Indian leaders suddenly remembered that there was another old graveyard on the other side of the road and that this would be moved if the Government paid the men who dug up the bodies. And there were questions of superstition. What about compensation?

Government replies continued to be friendly as long as a solution seemed to be in sight. But there was always a danger that someone might grow impatient. If this happened, the bulldozers would simply come through very early in the morning and push the edge of the reserve into the river. No one would be to blame. The Highways crews would say that they were only obeying orders and the officials would say that no order had been given and no one would ever discover the truth.

For the most part, the talks I had with Philip were about small things and were very instructive so far as I was concerned. As the weeks passed, I began to realise that the little world in which he lived was far apart, governed by intricate and complicated metaphysics which was untouched by my own thinking. Early judgments I made were false. There was poverty. There was sometimes drunkenness. There was a lack of formal education. But these things were relative to the alien culture. Within Hagwilget were deeper questions of prestige and class and faith and human relationships which could not be valued by an outsider.

Unlike the Tsimshian Indians of the upper Skeena, the Hagwilget people did not have a crest system for the control of marriage and inheritance. They had not at any time developed the long house and, in fact, had remained nomadic until the churches were built and the reserve system was introduced. But the village was divided into three or four families, each having a grandfather in command. Philip had a rival for the position of hereditary chief, and this was complicated by the fact that the priests had appointed a Catholic chief. All the expediencies of history were handed down as Indian custom, psychology or taboos whereas they were often the result of a white man's haphazard decisions. It did not matter much to me where the customs came from and, in the end, I concerned myself only with individuals. Philip was a man I liked. He was gentle, thoughtful and proud. He used to say: "Why are all white men greedy?" And he would wait for my answer with an expression of great innocence.

Many years ago, one of the priests had built himself a house on the hill near the church. Because it was not used, the band had taken over the house as a home for children whose parents were sick or lost or in gaol. This was the first such home in British Columbia, possibly in Canada. Its official opening started a series of battles against red tape which were unique. The struggles were with Federal bureaucrats, Provincial bureaucrats and Ecclesiastical bureaucrats.

Theoretically, the church owned the house, but this could be disputed because no one could claim ownership of buildings or artifacts on Indian land. A compromise was reached after negotiation. The Provincial Government agreed to subsidize the home because it was responsible for all child welfare programmes, even on the reserves. But subsidized homes were for children of all races and religious denominations, and the house at Hagwilget became an island where Catholic, Indian house parents were to look after white, Protestant children. And, for that matter, those who spoke the Carrier language were to care for children who understood only Tsimshian.

There was no limit to the possibilities, but we were not prepared for some of the difficulties. At first, the children placed in the home were native Indians and lived normally on the reserve. However, when they turned up at their usual school the Federal authorities refused to pay their subsidy. This matter of educational costs was complicated. The Indians had never paid property taxes from which derived the financial costs of the public schools. Therefore, when the children from reserves were sent to parochial or public schools, the Federal Government paid the bill. But they would not do this for our children in the home. The building, they said, was technically Provincial territory. It was treated like an embassy or a ship on the high seas.

We applied to the Provincial Government for some money. After several weeks, they replied that the children should not go to the Catholic school but should be sent to the ordinary public school. This was done, but a few days later the children were back in the Catholic school and the argument started all over again from the beginning. It turned out that one section of the Indian Act stated that no child could be sent to a school other than that administered by the religious denomination of the village.

All this dated back to the era when the missionaries made a verbal agreement to divide up the Indian tribes and not to poach for souls on one another's territories. Some of the missionaries only travelled to the Skeena area once or twice a year, and it was comforting to know that one's flock was intact, so to speak, until the next visit. School was very important in this matter, because some of the missionaries had not been permitted to enter the Indian villages and had made many conversions through the influence of the children.

We, however, were supposed to be living in the last quarter of the twentieth century. There had to be some solution to the problem.

At about this time, I had been given authority to order some kitchen furniture for the home. A suitable set of bronze tables and chairs were chosen by the house parents and the order was mailed to Winnipeg. A month later, we received a letter which regretted that there were no more bronze tables but that silver and white sets were on their way. Was this all right? Would we confirm the order by wire? We confirmed the order. Next day, a large crate arrived at the railway station and we moved it up to the village. It contained a bronze table and six bronze chairs. Three days later another crate arrived and was found to contain a silver table and six silver chairs. Next day, we received a letter from Winnipeg which regretted that they could not fill our order for silver tables and chairs but that bronze sets had been found in the warehouse and would be sent without delay. The third set of tables and chairs eventually arrived. Almost the same thing happened when we ordered an electric saw for use in the home and received saws every morning in the mail for six days. After that, we spent many happy hours looking through the catalogue, planning what we should order before the computer in Winnipeg finally blew its main fuse.

Bureaucratic tangles into which the various administrations worked themselves were of constant interest to Philip and his friends. He took little part in the negotiations, but his memory was good. He was still demanding payment for something that had happened in 1925. All the white officials concerned were dead or had retired. Many of them had made promises which were unauthorised and impossible to keep. For instance, when a rock was blown up in the centre of the river, the Indians protested that this would make it more difficult for them to gaff salmon. The official said that if this was the case, salmon would be supplied to the village. Philip remembered the promise and he remembered the name of the official. Of course, the rock had been blown up. No salmon had been supplied.

Philip took a fatherly interest in the developments on the reserve; he approved of the children's home, because he knew that the future of his grandchildren was at stake. One of the fruits of progress in the district was a brand new liquor store. Most Indians, whose lives were hard and whose homes were not particularly warm or comfortable, enjoyed social drinking. There were few, if any, Indian alcoholics. Many did not drink at all. As in all communities, there were some who drank too much. If an Indian was drunk on the street he would neither feel ashamed nor guilty. He might even feel heroic, because wine had dimmed his innate sense of inferiority. Certainly, he was unselfconscious.

New arrivals in the district, particularly those model citizens who only drank at home, paid their taxes, owned two cars and a new house, kept their adulteries quiet and went to church on Sunday, were very critical of the Indian parents. It was perfectly possible for someone to report an Indian to the magistrate and for the Indian to be put on the interdict list. In course of time, the Indian would receive a letter which would disclose that he was on "the list". This meant that he could not buy liquor or even be found possessing it. This was a form of prohibition applied to individuals without trial or warning. If, subsequently, the man was seen in a beer parlour or found with a bottle of beer in his car, he could be fined. If he could not pay the fine, he was sent to gaol. No time was allowed for the fine to be paid.

Under these circumstances, it is not surprising that the Indian men and women were well represented in the local gaols. Often, both parents were sent away on the same day and no one cared very much what happened to the children. Interdiction was removed from the statute book, but by that time much harm had been done. Indians had accepted the fact that they might go to gaol simply because they could not pay a fine. They had become accustomed to a form of injustice which still persists, a legal discrimination against the poor. To plead guilty, one might say, had become a habit of the native people.

I had become concerned about the fate of the children. If lucky, we would get a little warning that the parents might be taken from the village. More often, I would walk into a house to find a twelve-year-old girl cooking a meal for her younger brothers and sisters. If there was an infant, he or she would have been taken to the house of a married sister or an aunt.

In the past, we had usually put the children in a foster home which meant that they had to be identified before a judge and, within a reasonable period of time, would be made wards of the Superintendent of Child Welfare. When the parents came back, the process of returning the children to their homes would start. There was a new court hearing. Sometimes the foster parents would be very angry, thinking that we were sending the little boys and girls back to some kind of ghetto. The magistrate might question our actions. Did we think the children had the same opportunities at home? What about education? What was their home life like? Were the parents responsible people?

It was very difficult to explain that we were not in court to alter the destinies of the Indian children but had simply been looking after them when the parents were away. Could we have explained that the whole problem derived from lack of communication and understanding? Home was home to any child. The native families were not worried by status symbols. The condition of home life on the reserves was accepted by Federal health officers who had very limited budgets and hoped to keep their jobs.

It was to avoid the endless move from reserve to foster home and from court to court and village to town and school to school that the priest's house at Hagwilget was converted to a children's refuge. Sometimes the Chief Councillor, the elected chief, would admit children for reasons of his own. People came from distant reserves to look over the place. We had endless problems with the lighting, with the plumbing, with the furnace. But the old house beside the church became warm, alive. There was always a bunk bed available. There was always something to eat there. The roof did not leak and the rooms were warm. There was no emotional tension. What did it matter if the stair carpet was threadbare and the window in the kitchen cracked? Who cared if there were drawings on the walls? Was it important if the house parents had no university training and had never heard of Doctor Spock? The children didn't care, and that was the main thing.

The people of Hagwilget laughed as much as they wept, and this meant that they had courage and endurance; they had an oriental fatalism, a sense of following their ancestors, and the Irish worship of death was felt rather than seen. Even when some of the laughter was from the east, derision in the face of death or disaster, there was no tension. I used to come from one of the Hagwilget houses and feel as if I had been on holiday. Perhaps it was that there was no real necessity to speak, to choose words, to impress, to explain, to apologise. Everything was understood, including my own limitations and weaknesses. Love and hate and jealousy and anger were excused, because they were part of a person. But greed and ambition and hypocrisy and interference were dismissed as silly perversions of the spirit.

So, I would bend my head and walk out into the blinding sunshine of the northern summer and feel strong after an hour with quiet, perceptive people. The mood might last for an hour or two, but it would wear off. The effect, however, was cumulative, and life became easier as the weeks passed.

As one turned off the black highway on to the reserve road, a cloud of white dust would rise behind the car and the springs would groan and it was necessary to change gear to drive up to the church. From the top of the hill you could look west down the valley of the Skeena, which was a soft green between the mountains, and in the distance were the white peaks of the Seven Sisters.

It was a week day, very hot and dry. Some of the children had climbed down to the banks of the river to fish for trout. Men and women were sitting on the steps outside their front doors. The man who stepped out into the road to stop the car had his own special problem. Could I do something about Aunt Ellen? What was the matter? He told me that Aunt Ellen had died and should have been buried but the priest had not arrived and the body had swollen and was threatening to burst open the coffin. I asked what he had in mind. Could I go down to the store and buy some hemp or sisal rope with which the coffin could be bound? Was this needed at once? Yes, he said. There was no time to lose.

I drove four miles down to the store and bought some rope and returned to the village. After Aunt Ellen was safely roped, it was possible to continue routine discussions. One of the women asked if I could find her eighteen-year-old daughter, who was either in Victoria or Vancouver. No one could find her. But, from time to time, she was seen, a shadow passing or a face in a lighted doorway. She did not write, but someone had brought a message. "Please come and take me home."

How did one find a girl in a city? What sort of life would she be leading? Sometimes one of the young women would turn up in gaol or in hospital, but they were always released and discharged to the streets. It was never anybody's responsibility to ask questions. A few Indian girls were living in Chinese communities, their hair cut short, their names changed. Once, when an old house caught fire, four girls were brought out who had been locked indoors for over two years; they could hardly see in the bright sunlight. These young people were the early victims of social progress, of integration. There was no point in considering the general situation. But there was reason to look for one girl. Often, valuable information came back through the grapevine, the intricate network of communication existing in and between Indian communities and between the groups in the larger cities.

However, if I wanted to see Marion it was necessary to leave the village and scramble down the overgrown trail to the banks of the river. Old, ruined Indian homes were crumbling in the long grass. The river was low, and the children fished from the rocks. Marion was Philip's daughter; she was responsible for the fact that the family ate well. She grew vegetables, had shot a moose when the men were away, had shot a bear by mistake, and she knew how to catch rainbow trout in the lake behind the reserve.

I used to drive up to the lake in the summer evenings and take with me a fly rod and a box of flies, my net and all the usual equipment recommended for hooking and landing a fish. There was a small boat on the beach, and it was very pleasant to drift out on the water and watch the fish rising. Marion was contemptuous of my efforts, and one evening I went out with her to see how she fared. We rowed across the lake to where the trees leaned over the water and there were shadows under the bank. Marion had a short line, four or five feet long. She put salmon eggs on the hook and threw the bait towards the shore. Her head moved, and I rowed quietly towards the south, following the curve of the lake. Marion kept the salmon eggs off the bottom by moving her right hand in circles so that the hook began to dance and jerk and the salmon eggs swayed through the speckled sunlight. It all seemed very easy.

We caught three good rainbow that night, but I was

never converted to her methods and continued to use my fly
rod with poor results.

In winter time, Hagwilget almost disappeared into the snow
fields except that the white houses became yellow and the
road up the hill was crowded with children on toboggans. It
was even more difficult to reach the church. On one occasion,
I parked my car on the slope and it was blown down the
green ice and went through the wall of an empty house at
the bottom.

Once the land was frozen, the men went away to the
logging camps and sawmills and the young women remained
inside with the children. Some of the houses had electric
light but many of them were still lighted by pressure oil
lamps which gave out a steady hiss and a great brilliance.
The oil lamps hung from a nail, and I often knocked them
to the ground with my head. Heat was provided by round
airtight stoves which were usually very thin so that it was
possible to see flames through small holes. The stove pipes
wandered upwards and eventually went through a hole in
the roof. If the pipes were badly joined, which was often the
case, sparks would fly out into the attic, and the whole house
would be reduced to ashes in a few minutes.

The economy of the village was complicated. Ten years
before, the people could have supported themselves and, in
fact, did so. Their diet was simple. Their needs were few.
But they lived virtually without education or medicine or
security. Infant mortality was high. The expectation of life
for the men and women was almost half that of the white
population. It seemed, for a time, as if the benefits of the
European world would never cross the intangible line
between the new towns and the old reserves. Perhaps some
of the missionaries feared the results of contact. Eventually,
the more progressive agents from Ottawa demanded that
the native Indians be helped in their agriculture and
housing. This particular decade was a period of disruptive
change. The same people who advocated education and

wage earning for the young Indians went around complaining that the pastoral economy had been abandoned. They also objected when the Indian left his job to plant vegetables or catch fish. The administrators from the south were schizophrenic; they did not know what they wanted.

The result was that the Indians themselves became uncertain and lacking in direction. Few of the Indian Superintendents knew whether they were expected to spend more money on the reserves or protect the taxpayer. Philosophies and policies changed. An easy going and progressive administrator would be succeeded by a man who imagined that the less he spent the more definite would be his promotion. After ten years of expanding financial help for Indian people, experts were sent out into the field to find out why the people had become dependent. It is probably true to say that no working day passed in a three-year period when there was not a conference being held somewhere on these problems. Often the same men were on three or four different committees in a month, all the aims and resolutions being contradictory.

It is hardly surprising that by the time I reached Hagwilget no one was very interested in discussing government policies or decisions. Nearly every hour spent in that little village was filled with desultory conversations about children, parents, aunts, uncles and neighbours. The good and the bad and the indifferent in human relationships were all there. Every virtue and vice found in a city of a million people was represented.

The portrait of a village can only be a true portrait if it includes studies of every individual living there. The thoughts and hopes and fears of the people matter more than the wider significance of their collective predicament. We know, of course, that the Indian village has been engulfed by the alien competitiveness and pragmatism. It is very easy to simplify. The first impression is that the old peasant is dreaming of the past and that youth is corrupted by the mammon philosophy and that the successful or educated

Indian migrates to the city and wears a suit. This is not a true picture.

I remember going into one of the houses on a hot summer day when the shadows were welcome and the silence of the room was pleasant after a long drive on the mountain roads. We sat around the kitchen table. Someone was telling me about a bear that had been shot from the kitchen window when it tried to enter the smoke house. There was a story about drinking and fighting on a train which brought the older children home from residential school. One of the men spoke of the village school which had been closed and was used as a house by a government official. Was this right?

I had with me a small tape recorder and wished to confirm the correctness of some of the native singing. At the time, the children were coming home from school, wandering up the grass path in the summer heat. We could look out from the half darkness to the blinding rectangle of the doorway and see the small figures becoming distinct as they grew near. I switched on the tape recorder and listened again to the drum beat and the strong voice of an old man. The effect was electric; it was immediate. Everyone started to smile, and the children threw down their books and began to dance. They danced into the house so that the dust flew up from the wooden floor. Their bodies moved back and forth and their feet pounded in time with the drum. People came running over from the other houses, and I felt as if the whole community was coming around after being anaesthetised. And when I switched off the tape recorder the laughter continued like an echo, and the children stared at one another as if wondering what had happened.

Not far away, on the other side of the church, there was an old grey house which consisted of one room and an attic. It must have been a cold place in which to live in winter time, for summer winds would blow through the walls and send spurts of dust up through the floor boards. Once the snow came, there was reasonable insulation, but if there was an early drop in temperature, no stove would keep out the cold. The room was crowded, and whenever I went in there the grandmother was in bed. There were three beds in the room, and the space left was just enough for the table, the heating stove and a wood stove for cooking. The table was the only flat surface and it was used for everything from eating to storing plates and doing bead work.

The granddaughter lived in the attic, and it was her home. She climbed up a ladder and through a square hole and reached a space from which it was possible to see the sky through shrunken cedar tiles. Her parents travelled throughout the north, working in logging camps and sending money home when they could. One day, she had come to me with tears in her eyes and had asked if I could find her another place to live, a foster home or a boarding home in the town.

We sat and discussed it behind the house where there was an old shed for storing wood and bear skins, snow shoes and bits of old bicycles. I said that I would see what I could do, not taking her request too seriously. The girls who went to the public school had to suffer oblique and bitter insults from the white children, who never tired of asking what was in a lunch bag or if a dress had been handed down or why some children were allowed to come to school with lice. Such cruelty was common; it even became a necessity to preserve self-esteem which was often in short supply. It was, for some people, nice to know that there were some who were worse off than they were themselves. In fact, the integration of schools was a real blessing to some of the white children whose parents were poor.

The granddaughter knew that a ward of the government was given a clothing allowance and would receive an adequate lunch from the foster mother. She also knew that she would be in the comparative bright lights of a town of three thousand people. She was young, but she may have had a lover. She knew all about alcohol. Somewhere in the day to day complications of her life in two worlds, she had reached a point of desperation.

Whatever she expected, she would be disappointed. The disenchantment sprang from her own temperament, from pride and lack of understanding. It was just a matter of time before she would ask to return home. However, as we sat in the sunshine and watched the shadows change on the mountain, a whole new world opened up for the girl. Some of her friends were in town. She could not, in any case, envisage the detailed business of foster home life. She did not realise that those who are usually accepted as foster parents are middle class and outwardly puritan, many of them having an almost fanatical dedication to the future of the children placed in their care.

After she moved, I saw the girl from time to time, sometimes on her way home from school and sometimes by the lake where we bathed. Months passed, and I saw her on the ski slopes. When I went to the foster home she was quiet, almost serene. She was obedient, polite, punctual. But she never laughed; she refused to make friends; she did not confide in her foster mother. Later, she phoned me one night and I met her in the street where she said she had been drinking and leaned on my car sobbing so violently that I almost took her to the doctor. She wanted to go home. More than anything in the world, she wanted to go back to her little attic room at the top of a wooden ladder.

The date was arranged, and whenever I visited the foster home I would see her calendar on the wall with a red square inked around the day of the month when she would be driven back to the village. When I collected her on the last day, she walked out of the house without her newest clothes and her skis and all the possessions that foster home life had brought to her. She did not look back, and at no time on the sixty mile drive did she mention the people she had stayed with or the town or that other life she had experienced.

We drove into the village. It was a cool day with light snow falling. The girl jumped out of the car, her head bare and her hair flying out behind her as she ran up the slope and then rolled in the snow with her dog and, presently, was engulfed in a gay, welcoming crowd of young boys and girls. She did not collect her luggage from the car, because she had forgotten about me as well.

# 6

# Babine

I GO to Babine in the spring. A long, steel lake with a low shore and the mountains barely visible. The bow of the boat points north. There are no roads along the water's edge, only the single gravel one which strikes the lake and stops. The final thirty mile boat trip is almost romantic; it leads away from the mechanical world. The only discordant sound is from the outboard. If you stop that, the water slaps the wooden hull for a moment. Then there is silence. A white and empty sky. Lake Babine. The farthest east of my territory and a place of loneliness, of serenity.

It can be rough. A cold north wind often blows down the lake and kicks up waves. It takes three hours or four hours or five hours to reach the village, depending on the weather. You can cut down the time when you know the lake, because you can take the shortest course. It is possible to go from point to point once you understand the geography. Babine may look straight on the map, but it twists its way to the north like a wide river. It is very deep, seven hundred feet in places.

Even on the hottest and calmest day, it is pleasant to sight the village, first a glitter of sunlight on windows. After the last corner, and still far away, the houses are on the eastern shore at a spot where the lake ends and the Babine River flows out into the valley. The village grows closer. Houses along the edge of the water and some up the slope, a church, the school. Nothing much to see. Flat-bottomed lake boats drawn up on the beach and a long dock near the Hudson Bay Store. Horses wander between the houses. Dogs and children running together.

Paul is with me, both as friend and interpreter; he looks at the place over his high, shining cheekbones, and I am not sure whether he is happy to be back. He has married a girl from another village and lives in the valley of the Bulkley River. He is young, perceptive, uncommunicative. He sits in the bow of the boat and watches the details become visible.

I turn my head to look back at the blue lake water and the jagged, far away skyline with the Babine mountains withdrawn and shadowed in an evening mist. To the north, the land is a wilderness of mountain and forest reaching up to the Yukon border. The hunters know it, and the trappers know it. The pilots of planes glance down at it and count the hours to a landing. A few prospectors wander back and forth in the everlasting quest. For me, it is only the far side of the skyline and the source of the wind.

"You going to stay with your father?" I ask Paul.

"I expect so."

We pass the village. The cabin in which I stay is down by the school, at the point where the hundred mile lake narrows between reeds and is a river. The cabin is built of logs and contains three small bedrooms and a main room with a wood stove for heat and a propane stove for cooking. There are three oil lamps.

When we reach the small, wooden dock below the school we are both tired. It is now the grey-blue dusk of mid-evening. Paul helps me carry the boxes of food, my typewriter and tape recorder. He stands silently by the door for a moment. We watch the trout rising in the river and then he says:

"I'll be down in the morning."

"Right."

"Going fishing this evening?"

"Not tonight."

I watch him go along the path to the village. There are no lights in the school. I remember hearing that the teacher had left, the young man who liked to shoot duck with a rifle, hitting them as they rose off the water. So the school is in darkness, and I am alone except for the horses moving outside.

It is pleasant in the cabin. Once the sun has set, the air grows colder. I light the lamps and the wood stove and unpack the food. I have a choice of three bedrooms, but they are all very much the same. Each contains a small iron bed on which I can unroll my sleeping bag. Each has pin-ups of girls in bathing suits or less, consolation for the lonely traveller. There is a small, wooden chair beside each bed.

The river sounds louder after dark. From the open door, I hear laughter from the village. A boat comes into the lake from the river, and I can see the men reeling in their lines; I can hear the sound of the reels.

I sit at the table between the stove and the lamp, planning the week ahead. I am there to write a script for the National Film Board. The task is to put the sights and sounds of the village on record, and one wonders where to start. In the past? Babine is the home of the old Hagwilget tribe, Carrier Indians who speak the Athabaskan language. The village was once a summer fishing camp for the nomads, and then a missionary built a church and opened the first school. Houses were built; but the Stone Age man was walking on the lake shore a century ago. Roof tiles and decorations for the church were carried along a trail all the way from the coast, from the mouth of the Skeena.

We cannot film history, because my instructions are to write about the present. I do not wish to make a film which is only a repeat of every other film I have seen about Indians, old men complaining and children with running noses and white men saying it was up to the natives to help themselves and experts talking about the need for involvement. I am thinking of a script which will bring out the bitter-sweet texture of Indian life. Alone, away from the intruders, the people can be gay and charming and fierce and independent, masculine and feminine and young. They can be immensely wise when solving their own problems in their own way. Let the white man come to the village and the gaiety is unseen, the wisdom is simply a cultural more, the charm is irresponsibility and the fierceness is hostility. The distortion is very great; it has twisted every relationship since the first contact.

I put some wood in the stove and make coffee. There is a large steel plate over the propane burner, so I can fry the eggs and bacon on the flat surface. The cameras, tape recorder and typewriter are on the table. A pad of white, quarto-size paper. Six black-and-white films. A carton of cigarettes. A bottle of brandy . . .

I usually awoke at daybreak when I was living in the cabin. It was still quite cold the first hour after sunrise. There was a mist on the water. The window looked south, towards the village, and the stillness was supreme. No movement. No sound. No chimney smoke. It was possible to see the sharp lines of the boats as they angled upwards away from the water, dark silhouettes. By that time, I had grown used to the sound of the river. The water moved under the dock where my boat was tied up, and a duck went past, floating tail first into the shadows under the willows.

I had my first cup of coffee of the day, which was the best. Outside, the mist rose, and sunlight came through the treetops. Overhead, the sky was blue. About half past nine, two children and a dog wandered down along the path from the empty school; they were coming to see me, but their course meandered; they were diverted by anything of interest.

The little girl arrived first; she was about ten and wore a sweater over a thin, yellow dress. Her black hair was long. She stood in the doorway without speaking while her eyes took in the cabin. Her brother, he looked like a brother, remained outside, holding the dog by a rope collar.

I said: "Hi. Like some coffee?"

She observed me with caution.

"Coffee?"

"No."

I lit a cigarette and looked out of the window to where the mist was burning off and the water rippled by the morning breeze. The children watched me; they did not find speech necessary. I was their entertainment for the moment. From their expressions, it looked as if they expected me to turn into a frog or vanish in a cloud of blue smoke. After a while, I said: "I've been here before."

"My mother wants to see you," the girl said.

"I'm on holiday."

"My mother wants to see you."

"Do you ever have a holiday?"

She shook her head.

"You're on holiday now, aren't you?"

"Yes."

"Oh, well . . ."

I found my camera and put in a film. The little girl came up to the table and watched with black, astounded eyes; she had only two answers to my questions, neither of which was very revealing. I said:

"I want to take your photograph."

"Yes."

"Will you come outside?"

There was a pile of firewood in front of the cabin. Beyond that, the ground sloped to the lake shore. The children were unselfconscious, even bored. They had delivered their message and were interested in returning home; they had exhausted their curiosity. I took two pictures and said: "Thank you very much."

There was no urgency in the first hours of the day, and I sat in the sun and watched the children as they walked along the trail. On the far side of the river, the country was flat. I could smell it, the scent of sage and pine and all the dead wood and dead leaves becoming warm in the spring sunshine. The children were no longer visible, but the sound of their voices came with clarity across the stillness.

The church stands at the top of the slope above the village and on the edge of the trees. In some ways, it is the visible symbol of the Indian reserve; it is a monument to the missionaries who travelled hard and worked hard in the days before the road and the plane and the civil servant. The roof of the church is covered by squares of tin on the inside, and the effect is one of elegance and richness. The sun glitters through the windows. There are some dead flowers in a vase. A smell of old books. Cobwebs in the angles of the walls. The priest arrives once or twice a month unless someone dies or two people want to be married.

Behind the church there is a trail which leads thirty miles through the bush to Takla Lake and to the country of the Arctic watershed. The old village is below, but there are three houses in the trees near the church. One belongs to the priest, one is empty, the owner having killed himself, one is obviously occupied. At the side, a smoke fire burns under a moose hide. A second hide is stretched on a frame. The bloody and fly-covered skin of a large beaver hangs on the wall.

The kitchen is filled with confusion. A working room. A bird, it looks like a grebe, lies on the table. Plates and saucers, bags of flour, knives, guns, fishing gear, toys, clothes and part of a snow shoe. The possessions of a large family have somehow been absorbed into the small house. One is conscious of iron beds everywhere, back to back. Henry smiles and makes a rather old-fashioned bow; he tells me the story I have heard many times, of how the Hudson Bay store has refused to collect supplies from down the lake and has increased the price of sugar and flour and tea and coffee. There is not enough of anything. We sit together on the front steps and stare out over the village to the lake and the faint blue of distant mountains and the dark forest still half hidden in the morning haze.

"I'm on holiday," I say.

Henry ignores this, for he is not willing for me to change my identity to suit myself. He continues to give me an account of his life as it is lived under the wet blanket of a Federal administration which intrudes into every aspect of his existence. He has forgotten when this was not so.

"What is life here like?"

"Oh, all right. Quiet, you know. Not much happens."

"You haven't thought of leaving?"

"No. I've always lived here."

"It's very beautiful."

"Yes," Henry says. "Very quiet."

After a moment, I tell Henry that someone is going to make a film of his village, and he looks interested for a brief moment. Then he says:

"You staying here long?"

"Five days."

It is one thing to escape from the town and have a holiday in a silent place on the lake shore. It is something quite different to live at Babine. Those who are sick have to travel down to the road's end by boat. They have a drive of forty miles before reaching hospital. Most survive. In winter time, when the lake is frozen, travel is faster but less safe. The houses are old; few of them have water piped to the kitchens. Many of the roofs leak, and if a window breaks glass has to be ordered from outside. There is no electricity except in the school. One man is blind. One young man, almost a boy, lies curled up on a bed in half darkness, slowly withdrawing into a private world of his own dreams.

Henry's daughter comes up the winding trail from the store; she is a tall, slim young woman of twenty. Henry ignores her, and the girl smiles at me as she passes. It would be very bad manners for her to interrupt the conversation I am having with her father. Presently, she comes out of the house and sits on the grass, slightly behind us, enjoying her own private circle of sunlight. It is a few minutes before Henry includes her in the talk.

"Have the supplies arrived?"

She shakes her head, and I am aware that she is laughing at me or with me. Six months ago I found her a job in town and she worked as a housekeeper. It was in mid-winter that she suddenly became impatient with her new life and vanished, travelling in her own secret way until she reached home. Her employer was very angry and gave me a long lecture about the lack of ambition of Indian girls.

"What are you doing with yourself?" I ask her.

"Oh, I don't know. I trapped my first beaver."

"You didn't like the town."

"Not much."

"What went wrong?"

She puts her head back and looks at me over the top of her cheekbones, a gesture of impatience. "They were silly. And they never paid me. Always promising."

"You didn't like them?"

Her voice is very soft. "Those white guys gave me nothing but promises."

There is no point in saying anything. It is all probably true. The impact of a competitive and materialistic society on the young woman from Babine is one of disenchantment. The families who took in the native girls were always buying houses and cars and television sets and boats and cameras and rifles. Somehow, there was never anything left over for the girl.

"Didn't they pay you anything?"

"Just the first two months. Then a week here and there. It doesn't matter."

It may not matter to the girl but it matters to me. So many things go wrong with the fragile little plans we have to make the young people less vulnerable. I remember one girl who went away from the village to work and was seduced by the man of the house. The man's wife knew what was happening, but she only laughed and shrugged her shoulders. If it had been a white girl, she would have worried. But an Indian girl. . . .

Henry accepts a cigarette. "Not good. Those people."

"I'm sorry."

"There's not much work around here."

"Just logging."

"Yes. Some logging down near Old Fort."

I am looking down on the small houses and the lake and the dark trees along the shore. It is possible to see the day's activities taking place, developing from mid-morning in their timeless way. The men take boats up the river and return with logs. The women wash clothes and scrape moose hides and smoke fish. Boys cut wood for the stoves. This is the business of survival. The people prepare for the winter; they think about food and warmth and the means of getting from one point to another through the snow. What would happen to Babine if all the men went away to earn money?

It is time to move. I press my cigarette into the soft ground, unsling my camera and take a few random shots from the hilltop. If I adjust the focus and swing around casually to my right, I can take a picture of the girl who observes me with placid disdain. And then she laughs.

"You shouldn't waste film on me."

"I want to find someone who can sing the old songs."

Henry says: "Many people here sing the old songs. Duncan knows them. And Dick. You know Dick?"

"Yes."

"You know where Duncan lives?"

"No."

"I'll show you if you like," the girl says.

We all stand up, and I shake hands with Henry. Downhill, the path winds between trees and comes out near the southern end of the village. The girl walks ahead of me; she leads me to a small cream house. An old man sits on a chair outside the door, and I hear the girl's voice and the incomprehensible, guttural replies. I am ignored. Negotiation takes place with all the oblique protocol of high diplomacy, and I sense that the girl is being treated with the sardonic contempt an old chief might have towards a member of the new generation. Presently, the girl turns:

"He will sing the songs for you. Tomorrow morning."

"Thank you very much."

Duncan's lined face changes; it softens. At one moment I am conscious of the cruel and inscrutable mask. Then the old man smiles. He says:

"You come. You come tomorrow."

It is important to remember that even if the village at Fort Babine is a small place and far from the nearest road, it was once on the main trail from the Naas River to the interior. One of the first trading posts was at Bear Lake, to the north. In summer time, when the fish known as oolachan were thick in the rivers, the Indian people carried the fish down from the north to Kitwancool and Kuldo and Kitsegas, Hazelton and Bear Lake. Since then, Kitsegas has been abandoned, Kuldo's log houses cannot be found and the last family to live at Bear Lake struggles to survive each winter. The old trail is lost in the shadows of the rain forest.

Charlie comes from Bear Lake and considers Babine to be overcrowded and suburban. He takes his dug out canoe up the river every evening, and I have often suspected that he keeps his home brew in the bushes on the right bank. Today he sits indoors and brings out some of his old treasures, pink clay once used by the girls to paint their faces, some old knives, bear skins, a long-barrelled rifle. He sits on a stool in the middle of the room and talks with great contempt about the new generation.

"I'm Bear Lake Charlie. I tell you. I remember. Bear Lake not like this place. Not like these people here. I was chief there for my people and we kept the law. One time I remember a man went mad in winter and killed a woman. We tied him up to a post and sent for the Mounted Police. But it was a bad winter. Police not come. The people tell me to shoot the man and we let him go and he ran out from the village and I ran after him and shot him. I never kill him with one shot and he crawled around like an animal for a while. Then the people tell me I should shoot him again. This time I kill him. That was our justice."

"What did the police say?"

"Oh, they ask here and there. I can't remember. They came in the spring."

"Do you like it here?"

"No. I come from Bear Lake."

"You don't like it here?"

"Too many white men here. Like you. What you want from me? You know, I'm Charlie. You want me to talk into your machine?"

"If you want to."

"My wife says to tell you the house is too small."

"Are you warm enough in winter?"

"Bah! You sound like the Indian Agent."

"What did the Indian Agent say?"

"He asks questions. He asks if we have enough to eat and I say we don't have enough and he smiles and says do we have enough to wear? He asks questions but never listens to what I say."

"You don't belong to this band?"

"This band? These people. No. But now it is different. They make me join the band to have a house."

Charlie would talk for ever, circling around his subject, using repetition to convince himself that I understand. He remembers a great deal. He is a difficult man, because his mind is in another century, and I have to make a tremendous mental effort to judge him from the antiseptic and mechanised century in which I live. I have to consider his justice, his art, his morality. Probably he is more skilled than I, a better hunter and trapper, a good husband and provider. He is a man who has accepted change for his children and grandchildren, never complaining about the generation gap of a thousand years. He is hard, determined. He would like to be immortal. Personal possessions are few; they are valued for their use. Affection is reserved for children, for a life of hardship and endurance does not permit love.

Charlie represents himself; he is an individual. He does not think or care about the other Indian tribes in Canada and North America; he probably knows that they exist, but he is not curious. He knows that he is not like white men; he is warmer and kinder, more cruel, prouder, braver, more cunning. He has suffered from lack of food, lack of shelter and comfort. It is a very simple and natural transition of innate skills, which once belonged to the hunter, for the purpose of obtaining canned meat from the Agent. The culture survives.

The anthropologists and sociologists might evaluate Babine, using their own distinctive variables; they would study a group. But Charlie and Duncan are individuals, of the same age but different in temperament, experience and abilities. Compared to a white man, they seem almost identical. Anthropologically, they share culture and language. Yet they are different men. They have different friends.

Charlie says: "You know Bear Lake? Good place. You do anything about our house, white man?"

"There are no other houses."

"There are no other houses."

"Isn't that true?"

"Yes."

I would like to see Charlie lying on the couch in the office of a brilliant, young psychiatrist. Charlie's normality is obvious. What else could he be? What else could he know? How else could he behave?

At this moment, I am a deer, a mule deer perhaps. Charlie is stalking me with his mind. I say: "You could go and live somewhere else? Hagwilget?"

"Hagwilget?" He shakes his head. "Small place, eh?"

"Small, yes."

"Any houses there?"

"We could find out."

The stove glows red. The old man's hair is plastered down by sweat. He is silent for a long time, thinking of some other place at some other time. He is not at all interested in the tape recorder nor in the world I represent. At one time, my mind would go far from the quiet melancholy of Indian homes and find itself in Paris or London with the lights and the roar of traffic. This was the simple contradiction of physical and mental presence. Now, I no longer dream of black against white. It is the old man who is in a house at Babine but has momentarily left me for somewhere I know nothing about and will never visit. I cannot go back into the past. But his mind, like mine, seeks contrasts.

He sits on a stool, light entering the cabin through two windows. His wife sits on the bed. Her feet do not reach the floor. She makes very little effort to understand me, because my language is strange, my face unexpressive, my manner restricted. She does not look at me.

Charlie cannot and will not see himself in relation to the world, in relation to Picasso or Pilate or John Smith; he has been a chief and a fine hunter and with these things he confronts the universe.

When I go out into the white, spring sunshine Charlie is left with his own thoughts. He returns to the dreams and memories of old age and is probably thinking of Bear Lake in summer time when, in the old days, he was the best guide. I see him through the cabin window, still sitting on his stool.

After the long winter, the grass between the houses is short and dark and slippery. There is a rotting duckboard down what might be called the street. Twenty houses are left, some built of logs, some frame houses painted yellow or blue or the common Indian Affairs red-brown. One hundred and thirty people live there. Those who leave, find squalid accommodation in one-room cabins on the outskirts of Smithers, where the sewage lies on the top of the swamp and even the yellow mud of break-up cannot absorb and swallow the garbage. And in Vancouver the Indian shadows move under the street lamps as the people go to cold and bleak rooming houses and the girls are given whisky by the new pioneers and the welfare cheque lasts for a week.

If I imagine a film of Babine it is a close-up portrait, the hands of a young man as he carves. Sixty seconds of a child's face. And I would like to see the boats crossing the river at dawn and the scarlet or yellow colours of the fall. I see a picture of people in their own setting.

It will be necessary to film the complete cycle of the year, because much changes when the lake is frozen and the snow is deep and the whole scene is incandescent under the blue sky. There are days when the wind blows snow up the lake so that the village achieves an even more impressive isolation. Nothing is visible beyond the last house. The people sit indoors and wait for a change.

However, on this spring evening the river flows to the north and the trout feed at the edge of the reeds. The colours are green and green-blue and brown, and the colour of distant hills is like the shadow of wood smoke on the sky. It is very still. There is no wind. And while I prepare my supper in the cabin a man comes down like an English farmer with a dog at his heels and asks if he can talk with me. The result is something of a monologue.

"It must be good town, this place. I tell Indian agent but he wouldn't listen. These no good people. Somebody hung for drowning a kid. I tell them. You people. You work. You work the ground and work the land. Every winter lots of money come. Now, no work this town and the other day one man say I report him. I say no. I never report like that. I told him how long he make home brew. I told him that. He been put in gaol Smithers one time. That's why I write to the Indian agent but he scared to come out."

"Do they sell the home brew?"

"Who? No. Just one time they do that. Just one time. I told them. They crazy these people here. My wife not dare sleep last night. Say to me, you strong man. Go around town and make town good, she say. My land all right. Before last year's snow I make it. It not in my name but I have two boys. It belongs to my boys. My two boys. And Indian agent tell me to make town a good place."

"Does he come up often?"

"Oh, yes. Sometimes. Sometimes every month."

"That's good."

"Lots of people go to gaol any time. That's why I'm scared. I can't run away. I can't walk fast. Somebody maybe drink and come in my house. Get drunk. Somebody hurt. That's why I'm scared. Nowhere to hide in my little house . . ."

This is the sincere complaint of a man who can remember better parts of the old days when the Indian knew more about the land than did the white settler, and the native villages preserved their own kind of discipline. He forgets hunger and the cold and the hard times before moose came west. He forgets the deaths of women and children and the men who died in solitary cabins and were eaten by pack rats. Perhaps his complaint is justified.

He watches me eat with dark, incurious eyes. And much later, when I unfold my sleeping bag on one of the iron beds, I think of the old man and his fears and wonder what sort of society he might have founded if the white man had not taken over.

The window is open. I hear the lake wind and the trees stirring, water rippling and the horses going north. Darkness in Babine is complete. Only the sky seems lighter, the seamen's night sky which brings to the earth a glimmer from the stars.

Morning. Sunshine and a cool wind. Duncan is proud and abrupt and incredibly strong for his age. He is dressed in his formal robes and has brought along a special skin to wear for the bear dance. Dick taps at a drum. I switch on the tape recorder, signal with one finger and the singing begins. This is Duncan's reality, because he has heard the

83

songs for most of his seventy-five years. The sound is harsh, not very musical, but the magic echoes out under the open sky. It is mainly the drum beat; it is exciting. Not far away, some young children start to dance with momentary frenzy and then subside in helpless laughter. After half an hour Duncan pauses while I change the tape.

"You want any more?"

"Don't tire yourself," I say.

"You want any more?"

"Yes."

"Lots more. I know all the songs. Old songs."

We sit in the sun but out of the wind. After the last drum beat dies away the silence is complete. This is definitely Duncan's day, because he is the only man who knows all the old songs. I feel very happy to have my tapes with me, for this will ensure that a tradition is preserved. Yet Duncan is exceptional, and the young Indians listen to modern music played on their transistor radios. In almost every house you can hear the repetitive beat of the groups beamed out across the mountains from Smithers. And sometimes there is a spoken message for someone in the village. Mrs Charlie's daughter is ready for discharge from hospital. The Hudson Bay stores have arrived. Would someone send a boat down to the landing? Messages twice a day on the air.

"What we sing now?" Duncan asks Dick.

Paul appears; he leans against the house in his slow, indolent way. The older men ignore him, but he refuses to be ignored. He says:

"Did you tell them about the film, John?"

"No."

"You might film the Bear dance."

"You make a film," Duncan says with some disdain and no curiosity. "A film here?"

"Yes."

"You want to film me?"

"If you like."

"I don't mind."

"Who wants to see a film of Babine?" Dick asks me.

"I don't know."

"You get paid for this?"

"Yes. Just for the writing. I don't make the film."

"You pay me?"

"No," I say.

"You're not worth anything," Paul grins.

Duncan is angry. "You. Why you come here? Go back to that girl you married. You not belong here."

Dick starts to tap with his knuckles on the skin drum. A few more songs are recorded and then Duncan decides that he has had enough; he goes into his house and closes the door. Paul shrugs. He looks at me:

"The boys are putting on a concert tonight. About eight thirty. Why don't you come?"

The messages come verbally or on small pieces of paper like illicit love letters. I cannot escape the village life, the intrigue and guile and face-saving. I visit one man at night. The house is almost on the lake shore so that the bow of the boat is a foot from the front door. There are no lights. Only two small rooms. It is cold out. No warmer within the space enclosed by board walls. The stove has gone out, and it is possible to see the night sky through one window. The man lies on the bed with his two small sons, who sleep restlessly. He gets up and lights an oil lamp and the faces of the children look almost pale against the blankets. We sit and shiver in the flickering lamplight, and I think with pleasure of my own cabin down the lake shore and of the coffee I will make later and of the warmth of the sleeping bag.

The man's wife is a hundred miles away in hospital. He is lost, immobilised. His firewood is running out. He is short of food. He goes to bed early to avoid using oil. He would like to visit his wife, to talk to her, to be with her. Who would look after the boys? The trouble is that his wife comes from another village and he has no relatives at

Babine. If his wife had been a Babine woman it would have been easy. There are tears in his eyes. Probably his masculinity is mocked and he is miserable. He is a good logger, but his job may now have gone to someone else. And the bill at the Hudson Bay will be over two hundred dollars. His voice drones on. The little boys sleep close together to keep warm. There is a black puppy in a box in one corner of the room.

I tell the man that I will try to find a girl who will look after the boys. As I close the door, the man blows out the lamp and climbs on to the bed.

The concert takes place in Dick's house. Women and girls have not been invited, for, in fact, this is a bachelor establishment, two men living together for convenience. Eighteen of the younger men sit on the beds. Four of the older men sit at a table and play cards. The musicians, two guitarists and one man with an accordian, have made themselves more or less comfortable on boxes; they have left a place for me and spend a lot of time tuning up while I adjust the tape recorder. There is no conversation, just a few Indian words spoken quietly until the music starts. The young men tap with their feet on the wooden floor and the rhythm is emphatic. This is the music of the new world. My Blue Heaven. One of the boys sings in a high tenor. The guitarists are skilled; they learn by ear. Sometimes they go down to Burns Lake and play for dances on the reserve. The room is warming up and cigarette smoke fills the space above the rafters. We listen and record, and everyone enjoys the light and the warmth and the relaxation and the forgetfulness. Who really cares about the uncertain future?

After midnight, we all go outside and the figures scatter towards their own homes. I see the lake lying between the trees and feel the wind from the north and am suddenly aware of the prevailing sadness of life in that place. The summer is like a smile on the face of the land. In winter time, the evenings will be blue and the air very still and cold and a man walking a few miles over the Takla trail will be at the edge of the world.

Either I am growing used to the temperatures or each day is warmer than the last. A few white clouds overhead. Because of the width of the valley, you can only see the very tops of mountains through the trees. Snow on the peaks very white under the sunlight. The river is brown. Two boats cross to the west, a horse swimming between them. Someone is using a power saw up behind the school.

If I walk through the village the script I am trying to write unfolds very naturally before my eyes. It is purely visual. A moose skin is stretched horizontally between posts, and an old woman sits on the skin and scrapes it with a shovel. A tall girl with black hair to her waist runs down the slope and stops in front of me. Her face is classical, half hidden eyes, cheekbones, a slight smile. I imagine the face on a screen, a close-up of expression and texture.

"When are you going out?"

"Tomorrow."

"Could I come with you?"

"Of course. Where are you going?"

"Prince George."

"I'll probably leave about noon."

"Thank you."

We part. Could we film the girl's journey and the facts and emotions of her destiny? As I see her now, she is a shy, beautiful and very human person. She is capable and sure of herself. Yet the time may come when, in the other world, only a drunken man would be seen with her. Who would wish to film that story? Who would want to watch it? It is better to concentrate on the myths and legends, on the handicrafts. Possibly I am being influenced by a spell, by the enchantment of an almost timeless life.

Late that evening, a boat comes up the lake, and it is nearly dark and very cold when the strangers arrive. I recognise the priest in the stern. A girl of about twenty sits on the centre thwart, huddled and stiff. They say they have been two days on the lake and have had to stop several times because of strong winds. We go inside and drink coffee. It is now dark. The stove is red. The cabin grows warm and the visitors start to thaw. Presently, the girl goes off to her home. The priest and I talk for an hour before he climbs the slope to his house near the church. Much later, Dick comes down with a message he would like me to deliver in town. He asks me to play the recordings of Duncan's songs and we listen to the drum beat, and the old man's voice while the wind murmurs in the trees.

Ten days later, I hear that Dick is dead. Too much grain alcohol. By that time I am back in the noisy, competitive, organised world of the town, but I cannot forget the quiet and dignified man who knew how to beat the skin drum.

## 7

# A Funeral in Winter Time

KITSEGUECLA lies on the south bank of the Skeena River. The village is shaped like a cross of Lorraine, its base on the river bank with roads leading up a slope where the school stands. The village is the home of about twenty-five Tsimshian Indian families; it has one or two unique peculiarities which the people fight or cultivate according to their mood. Kitseguecla can never be described as ordinary or dull or simple or pastoral. It was, and still is, a very complex little society of interesting individuals.

It is often difficult to perceive which part of a culture derives from indigenous and primitive source and which part has been acquired from invaders. The village of Kitseguecla demonstrates, more than any other, the division of customs. For instance: many of the older houses had been designed and built when the railway came through in

1912; they had a Victorian look with wide staircases leading to the upper floor. The church was built in the late nineteenth century: the school much later. The original missionaries were Methodists, but some of the people broke away to follow a Salvation Army preacher. At the turn of the century, the various tribes were swept by epidemic diseases. Two hundred Kitseguecla people died during one winter.

In those days, the people lived from day to day. The year was broken by the annual gathering for the salmon run and by the oolachan run in the Naas River. Social life was based on the clans or crests, and the winter months were spent in the village, feasting and carrying on elaborate rites connected with secret societies.

If you drive past Kitseguecla today, you will see a few totem poles, small modern houses, gravel roads leading away from the highway and young people waiting for the school bus. It is not unlike other communities of the north. The car owning generation has arrived. There is an elected chief and a band council. This comes within the first glance, the first visit. Summer tourists will see an empty village, the house windows boarded up, for the people will be away on the coast. In winter time, it is very different.

Government officials, people like the Indian Superintendent, find their work very difficult when they come to Kitseguecla. For one thing, the crest system still operates. The power of the elected chief is limited. The people have preserved their own hereditary system, and it does not matter very much what frustrated officials in Ottawa might say. If a chief dies his house is left empty. If a man dies, his wife returns to her own crest and the house goes to the son of the man's oldest sister. Very often, because of disagreements about this with the visiting officials, the house remains unoccupied.

The men, women and children who live in the Victorian houses or in the functional houses now provided by the government, use the school and the church, their cars, telephones, television and radios. They are technically efficient. But they remain apart. The year follows a traditional pattern. Summer is the time for fishing at Prince Rupert. In the fall, the families return home and the men might do a little logging. There are sports days. Religious meetings take place in January and February. When the snow melts, potatoes have to be planted. The emphasis is still on the gathering and preserving of food. What might appear to be a calculated improvidence is almost the reverse.

The snow falls; the fine, powder-like snow of mid-winter comes down from a dark sky. Even at noon, the village is a place of shadows. This is the territory which frightened and defeated many of the gold seekers on their way to the Yukon. It is a place in which one might hear the spirits of the hills. The atmosphere encourages superstition.

The dogs do not bark; they wander back and forth searching for the bones of moose. They have a wild look, and many of them have coyote blood, or the amber eyes of the northern wolf. The horses move all over the country in winter, fending for themselves and frightening night drivers on the new highway between Prince Rupert and Hazelton.

Half way through the afternoon a bell tolls from the top of the road, from the direction of the church. The bell is large and deep-toned; it hangs in the open on a platform outside the church. The sound is muted by the snowfall, but it is heard in the school where a young teacher sits at her desk and where the children grow silent and preoccupied. Some of the girls wear white bracelets to keep away the spirit of death, for it is the day of a village funeral.

Death is no stranger in the villages of the north. Yet the rituals of burial do not become commonplace. The Salvation Army captain may read the prayers and lead a hymn, but the feelings go back to the unrecorded years before the missionaries entered the Skeena valley. The dead man's possessions are often burned or buried with him. The body has an identity of its own. All available money, all available food, is dedicated to the feast. Just where the tone values of superstition end and those of Christianity begin are not defined. At any rate, there are many strange emotions washing through the village during the hours of the afternoon.

The young teacher senses the preoccupation of the boys and girls, a nervous excitement which keeps their minds from their books. There is almost no point in continuing the lesson. It is just another unusual day.

The less attractive parts of the village are hidden by snow. If you want a more detailed description, imagine brown wood houses with small windows and sheds filled with wood. Old bear skins hang on the walls. Derelict cars have been pushed away under trees. Everything piles up because it is expensive to haul away rubbish.

The men and women walk up towards the church, singly or in pairs, the edges of the figures blurred behind the falling snow. Half an hour later, the coffin arrives on an old green truck, young men sitting in the back, bare-headed and proud. The three-man band of the Salvation Army walks ahead of the truck. The wheels begin to spin in the snow. The young men jump to the ground and push, their feet sliding uselessly. The truck stops. Someone is sitting on the coffin to make sure that it does not slide to the ground. The bell tolls. From the church comes the sound of organ music, and the lights have been turned on. Night will come early.

This may be an ordinary day for the people of the village, because a funeral is a funeral and the road to the church is steep. Normally, you have to drive fast and with determination to reach the school. One hesitation and the wheels lose their grip. I am watching this scene from one of the older houses – the home of a grandfather with children and grandchildren scattered on the ground floor and in the space upstairs under the roof. There is little conversation. My host is an important man, partly because his wife is the chief of both the Frog and the Wolf crests. She has an unknown amount of power in certain parts of the valley and on the mountain slopes to the south.

Arthur is not going to the funeral. He is old, a patriarch, if you like. He always talks to me in his own language, forgetting that I only understand a few words. He worries a great deal, about one of his grandchildren who is going to school in Prince Rupert, about his horses, about his influence in the community, about money, about his son, who has a poor relationship with the Superintendent. It does not take long to find out that the older Indian is confused by the many worlds in which he is forced to live. He must consider the Indian traditions, the customs and habits of his heritage; he must consider the artificial world created by white governments, the reserves and band lists and hunting rights; he must remember that his grandchildren may not like either of the older worlds but like to live as educated and sophisticated people, their contribution to their country being an addition to cultural diversity.

Today, he is sitting indoors and watching a funeral. He says:

"They blame me for this death. They blame my family. I'm afraid that they might do something."

"What can they do?"

Arthur looks at me to see if I am listening properly or just talking. "It's the old way, the Indian way. They think my family caused the death. You know. You can do things if you wish a man dead."

"Witchcraft, you mean?"

"You call it what you like. They say we did it. Would you go to their chief and tell him it wasn't our fault. I'm afraid of him. He told me to stay out of the dead man's house. He told me that if I went back I would die and he would put my body there on the floor between the door and the window. He said I would die and he would put my body there."

"I'll talk to him if you like."

"Lots of them die this winter. Three. Maybe four."

"Accidents?"

"Oh, yes."

"How are you supposed to cause these deaths?"

The old man shrugs. "There is one way. Someone from the village dies, even a dog, and you take something belonging to a man and put it on the grave. Then he'll die."

"Does it always work?"

He laughs. "I don't know."

I am looking out of the window, watching my car become covered with snow. It would be nice to leave before it grows dark so that the long drive home would be simpler. Arthur takes one of my cigarettes. Presently his granddaughter comes in and throws her school books on the table. She is seventeen.

"Hi," she says. "How are you?"

"Fine. School all right?"

"I guess so. We've been doing the Battle of Waterloo. D'you know about that?"

"Only what I've read."

"Same here." She sits down in the corner, abruptly subdued by the old man's silence. She has come in a small, orange bus from the modern world of the public school and is now in the land of her parents. It has taken only half an hour to cross nine centuries.

Arthur returns to his fear. "You'll speak to him?"

"Yes."

"Today?"

"I'll go now."

"Thank you. I am afraid for my wife and family."

"Naturally."

"You speak to him."

"Will he listen to me?"

"If you talk he'll listen."

It is cold outside, and the snow is dry, like dust on my bare head. The coffin is in the church. The organ plays. The sound grows faint as I walk away in the direction of the home of the chief of whom Arthur is afraid.

I cannot hear the river, because it is frozen, contorted ice awaiting the spring. A child's face is pressed against a window. The dogs circle. Blood on the snow where a moose has been butchered. Women moving into the village hall to prepare the funeral feast. Faces on the totem pole picked out in white snow. A carved sea wolf grins beside a house.

The old man is at home. His wife is perpetually worried and dislikes her husband but has nowhere to go. She cuts the wood and smokes salmon and is something of a slave. The man sits on a stool and stares at the floor, and I hesitate, because it is incredibly rude to interfere with his private affairs. The conversation is nothing but my own voice and the wife's voice and the top of the man's head as he tries to withdraw from the room altogether. So I bring the talk around to the funeral and to Arthur and to the threat and the fear and the stupidity of village strife.

My very presence is an insult, because the hereditary chief of the village does not have to answer questions. The only advantage I have as a white man is that the chief will think me ignorant, not impolite. It takes him five minutes to make up his mind. He raises his head and looks at me, not with anger or curiosity or humility but with the flat observation of a wise old man for a young fool. He reaches across to a drawer and brings out a small, black notebook.

"You want some facts? Here. On January fourth my brother fell off the back of a truck coming down from Newtown. He died. There were others on the back of the truck. They didn't fall off. They didn't know why he fell. But he died."

"It was an accident."

"You tell me it was an accident? You were there?"

"No."

He turns a page. "My sister fell through the ice and drowned in the lake."

"Yes."

"You know another brother was shot?"

"Yes."

"Was that an accident?"

"Yes. It was a young boy who had the gun. You were at the inquest."

"I was there."

"Do you blame that little boy?"

"No. He was told what to do."

"What else?"

"My third brother. He died."

"He was old and sick."

"Yes? And did you see the body?"

"No."

"It was all bruised. All black."

"There must be some explanation."

"And what about me. You wait for me to die?"

"You may be afraid. Others are afraid too. That's why I'm here."

"What do they fear? Their brothers have not died."

"They worry about you. Your brothers all died naturally or by accident. You must accept that if you want to live in a happy village."

"I'm an old man. I don't harm anyone."

"Why don't you tell them that?"

The wife interrupts. "Could you tell them?"

"If you like."

The old man puts his book away. "It's always the same here, you know."

"You are the chief."

He shrugs. "Oh, there are a lot of chiefs these days. Government ones . . ."

"Aren't you the real chief?"

"Yes."

"Enough people have died here."

"Yes. People die here," the old man says. "Soon we'll all be gone."

"Was it always the same here?"

"Yes. Always the same."

The silence is not a happy silence, and I find myself thinking of the young girl who is studying the Battle of

Waterloo. It is all right to let my mind wander. The exhaustion I feel is physical, the result of staying still when my nerves are raw, the result of staying silent, the result of talking all day to men and women who can turn on and off their personalities like electric currents. At one moment you are in touch and then, in an instant, you might as well be alone on the top of a mountain. And the only way to renew contact is to sit very still and wait until someone includes you in the circle of thought.

The old man has receded from me; he is simply a rather shabby old man who sits in a leaning house filled with confusion and cobwebs. A few moments before, he had the authority of a hereditary chief, someone who could cast fear into the darkest corners of the village like a fisherman casting a net.

It is colder outside, but the snow has stopped.

The children have gone home. The young teacher hands me a cup of coffee. We sit in silence at opposite ends of the table. It has been a depressing day for us both, and across the still, white village comes the wail of the mourners like the sad cry of a hundred curlews.

Later, there will be the feast and a certain amount of drinking and some hours of the night will be forgotten and the children will stay awake and be late for school in the morning. The teacher accepts this without complaint, because she has never imagined that school can replace all traditions and customs.

The grey light of day persists, but it will soon change to dusk when the cold creeps across the valley so that the forest is filled with the snapping of trees and the dull throb of sound carried for miles and of unknown source. This strange vibration is what constitutes silence in the north; it is made up of snow rustling, trees bending under a new weight, animals moving in the darkness, water under the river ice, and one's own heart beating.

The sound of the bell comes again. This time it is being

rung in a frenzy. A man shouts. The people are streaming back from the graveyard. Fire! Fire! We see smoke rolling across the snow and know that one of the little wooden houses is burning. There it is. Already, the roof is a ring of flame and the windows are filled with the yellow-black smoke. The teacher says: "What about the children?"

It is useless to run in the snow. Boots sink deep if you go off the path. Flames are shooting out of the house at all angles and the men and women step back from the heat. I ask a few questions. The parents were at the funeral and the children were alone for a while. They are all safe. They are standing with their mother who weeps silently as she watches her new home vanish. The roof falls in. Men are throwing buckets of water over the walls of the nearest house and the walls steam. The fire hose is useless, because the hydrant is frozen. There is nothing anyone can do but comfort the children who shiver and stand in the snow with bare feet. They will need clothes and a home for the night. They will need food and warmth and a refuge from the bleak moments when the excitement has died away and the loss becomes more tangible. For a short time, the heat from the burning house gives everyone a false sense of well-being. And, in a bitter way, it is lucky that I am there, because it is a very easy thing for me to put the children in the back of the car and drive away to the store some miles to the east. I can authorise clothes and food, ask relatives to help. And the village will work things out in its own way. The hours pass. It is dark when I leave the group of houses and start my eighty mile drive home. The funeral feast has started. Lights come from the village hall as figures move towards the building where memories will bring companionship and companionship will lead to forgetfulness and the hours of the night will be spent far from my own pragmatic world.

I returned to the village eight days later. The man whose house had burned was wandering down the road, and his wife sat on a wood pile. The sun was shining, but the air was cold. It was one of those winter days when the snow is as blue as the sky and the mountain slopes shine like silk so that the trees are finely etched against the backcloth by a Chinese artist.

The man was depressed. We walked up to look at the ashes of his home. There was very little to see except a black patch in the snow with footprints going in all directions and two dogs sniffing in the ruins. He told me that he could not stay where he was, because there was no room in the house for two families. He was a member of the band but he had been born farther north. He had married a local girl. He did not really like the Gitksan people, and thought it might be better if he left the reserve and tried to rent a house near the railway tracks which passed thirty miles to the east. There was one empty house which belonged to a cousin who lived in Prince Rupert.

We went to look at the house. It was very old, built of logs and weathered to a pale grey. There was only one room, and there were holes in the roof. The door was broken. But it was a house. It was possible to imagine the stove roaring and the windows curtained and the table set for a meal. The family would have their own home, a refuge from the acidity of village life.

We made a list of materials needed to keep out the snow and the wind and turn the old building into a suitable home for a man, his wife and their six children. It was never likely to be suitable so far as the Health Inspector was concerned. There was no water. Practical things like sanitation and impractical things like privacy were never a consideration anyway. The Indian families did not like houses divided into rooms because there was usually only one heating stove and the bedrooms became cold. Also, one oil pressure lamp hanging from the ceiling could light the whole house if there were no partitions.

A week passed. The Indian Superintendent had sent away for permission to spend 480 dollars and, after receiving a favourable reply, he had asked for tenders from three local building firms. Another week passed. Then the replies came in, and the lowest bid was ten dollars over the amount authorised. Another letter had to be sent to the Regional Office, and the homeless family wandered on the icy village roads listening for the sound of the truck bringing wood and nails and glass for the windows.

In the end, the truck did arrive. The family moved into the old, grey house. The stove was lighted. Plywood covered the holes in the floor. I drove down to visit them one day when the snow had returned, and wind blew up the valley. Even the dogs were sheltering under the houses. It seemed a long walk from my car to the door of the little log home when the outside temperature was thirty below zero and the snow was blown from the ground in an opaque mist. But it was warm inside. The children were laughing again. They sat on the beds and looked at the Christmas catalogues and dreamed impossible dreams. Their father was a man once more, head of his own household.

In summer time, the tourists would drive past; they might stop to take a photograph of one of the totem poles. They might even have time to notice that the houses were old and shabby and they would probably be surprised to see the children laughing as they ran together in the heat of the sun or sat in the green shade of the cottonwood trees.

# The Coast

*

# 8

# The Far Side of the Wind

IT was possible for me to visit the Homalco Indian band and to return in time for lunch. When, each morning, I drove along the coast road between my home and the office, I could see the sea, islands and a formidable backcloth of mountains. From a distance of fifty miles, the mountains appeared to be solid and unbroken, but this was a false impression. Salt water inlets ran to the east and the northeast; they were dark, windy places populated only by a few logging communities. One inlet penetrated to the snow slopes and glaciers of Mount Waddington, beyond which lay the ranchlands of the interior. The Indian village was on the coast between two inlets; it was little more than a dent in the mountain, but there was some shelter from the strong winds from the north. There were days when it was calm near the village waterfront, but snow was blown in a line of cloud from a nearby peak.

Before I visited Homalco, I was informed by people concerned with law enforcement and by those interested in public and private finance, that the Indians over there were difficult. The evidence was often hearsay, and the stories were all repeated and exaggerated as they were passed from person to person. For me, the stories were encouraging. It meant that I could look forward to new friendships, laughter, stimulation, challenge. The more terrible was the reputation of Indians, the more pleasant I found them to be. Conversely, those who were judged to be successful, to have "made the grade", were often self-conscious bores in white collars and ties. This was only a criticism of my own viewpoint.

If you arrive by plane at the village and if it is a day in

summer time, you will see small boys diving twenty feet from the dock into the clear water. There will be two or three fishing boats tied up together and one winched up on the beach for repairs. There will be a colourful line of washing from each house. At first sight, you are visiting a cove on the edge of the Tyrrhenian Sea. Also, the smell of fish is there. The kelp dries out on the hot rocks above the tide. Men and women sit in the sun. The Catholic church is behind and above the houses; it is very white against the trees. The atmosphere is distinctly Latin. Homalco is a place where happy and obstinate people disregard the surrounding world of Nordic man.

This was the farthest point west to which came the Coast Salish Indians. They attempted to settle on the islands closer to the Pacific but were driven out by the Kwawkewlth raiders, who were better organised and more warlike. A hundred years ago, a few families broke away from a large tribe on the mainland and sailed north; they eventually formed the Homalco band.

There were usually a few children to meet the plane, or there were men and women with letters to be mailed. Sometimes a man would come down to see if there was an empty seat, free if possible, which he could occupy on his way to a job on the west coast. A mother might ask if I could take her child to the doctor. So, there were always minutes of conversation in the shadow of the plane's wing.

From the jetty, it was possible to look down on the boats and right through the water surface to the rocks and weed on the bottom. I used to pause on my way up the jetty and light a cigarette and lean on the scarlet rail from which the little boys jumped and dived. Behind me, the twenty houses of the village looked down from the curved, terraced slopes of the bay. There were trees behind the houses, and, above the treeline, the scarred rock of the mountain. From the air, of course, the nature of the land was visible in all directions, but once down in the cluster of wooden houses all horizons were reduced to the immediate and familiar skylines.

Fred and his wife and children lived in an attic. In order to see him, it was necessary to go through the main room in which lived another family and climb a ladder to the boards of the ceiling. These were the floor boards of Fred's home. There were two rooms. In one of them were a bed, a table and an old stove which was separated from the wood of the wall by a sheet of tin. There was no heating except for that which rose from below and much of this escaped immediately through holes in the roof. There was no privacy, either from the people below or from the children who were crammed together in a square space at the top of the ladder. Neither Fred nor his wife were members of the Homalco band and were forced to live anywhere there was room for them in someone else's house. As the family grew in size, tension became very great. The attic was certainly unfit for human habitation; it was unfit for anything because the entire house was old and mouldering and unsafe. It was not surprising that it burned down, and in fifteen minutes was reduced to a little heap of grey ash.

Fred was well informed about the more absurd aspects of Federal and Provincial administration. It had taken him a long time to have his children admitted to the school on the reserve. Now, he had nowhere to live and the Department of Indian Affairs refused to help because so far as they were concerned he did not exist. Both he and his wife had been born there, but that made no difference. So Fred and I sat in the sun and looked out at the blue sea and tried to remember if there was an empty house on one of the nearby islands. He was not particularly depressed, because he still had his fishing boat and could earn his living providing the boat was fitted with a new keel.

Houses on the reserve were not covered by fire insurance, because no company would become involved in such a poor risk. The loss was complete. Thus, Fred was again dependent on charity and local hospitality. But it was not easy for his wife to move into someone else's kitchen and eat someone else's food. Probably it had been different before the first child arrived, but that was six years ago. I do not know how many years Fred and his family lived in that indescribable attic, but it was never suitable or acceptable in this century. Nor was it better or worse than other homes on reserves. Conditions at Homalco were bad by any standard. And because the houses there must have been new at some time, the conditions were growing worse. Fred had complained. Other people there, who did legally exist, had been complaining for twenty years. The complaints were filed away in a distant office. This is in no way a criticism of the officials in local administration, because money for Indian housing was limited by political decision in Ottawa. Only in cases of severe distress or bad publicity were the limitations ignored.

So I left Fred with the understanding that he and I would search for alternative housing along the island shores or on the edge of the mainland forest. He remained sitting in the sun, probably reluctant to move away from the security of the village in which he had spent all his life.

The houses in the village were on two levels. Seven or eight were close to the sea, and there was a path between the beach and the cedar poles on which the houses were built. That particular path was narrow, usually muddy in winter, covered with freshly cut firewood and various unwanted things thrown down from the doorways. In the dark spaces under the houses hung washing, old fish nets, planks, parts of boats and rusty saws. There also lived the dogs. Above that first level of houses was a broad rocky path which led from one end of the village to the other and climbed up to the school. The higher houses looked down on this path, and a few were built on the rocky arms which enclosed the bay. No professional planner would have chosen such a place for a village, a fact which was responsible for some of the charm.

On a summer day, senses would be drugged with the scents of sea, forest and rocks, the smells of tar and paint and drying nets. A few of the families would be up north, fishing in the inlets on the true Pacific coast. Several girls were berry picking in the United States. Children, who had been away from home during the school term, had returned from the comparative sophistication of the cities to spend the summer with their parents. In fact, there was a continual and habitual coming and going by boat and plane. Nobody seemed to be particularly keen to remain for ever in the rich, white, glamorous world of Vancouver or Edmonton or Seattle. If, at first sight, Homalco was a jumble of shacks on the edge of a lonely strait, it was also home. It was the place where people were remembered.

One of the girls who had recently returned from a city job was sunning herself on the veranda outside the house. She told me that it was difficult to come home but that it was even more difficult to stay in Vancouver when she had no work. She had graduated from High School and had been away from the reserve since she was thirteen. Her eyes were half closed as she looked towards the powder blue of the hills. She thought she might leave. She thought she might stay. She liked it there. She hated it. In the end, she started laughing, unable to make verbal sense of her contradictions. Like many of the other young Indians, she had overcome the problems connected with racial prejudice; she had become integrated in a work force but had subsequently been faced with all the difficulties of the unskilled and untrained, the subculture of the poor. She had found little security and worked hard for the minimum wage which supplied only the meanest of lodgings and enough food to survive for a new day of work. The people she met lived from day to day, usually drinking to forget the realities of their lives. They lacked hope, one of the essentials. They lacked faith in themselves. And the girl had remembered Homalco with the nostalgia of a young adult when thinking of childhood. The Indian way of life was structured in that it was based on example and not on guidance. From the city slum, a remote, quiet coastal village must have appeared as a Shangri-La. So, the girl came home.

I sat beside her on the wooden step, and we were looking at the village, each of us with our own thoughts. I had long ago stopped thinking of Homalco as an Indian village in which the people were dramatically different. All questions of anthropology and culture seemed contrived and unimportant. Each individual was passing through a moment in his or her life, and when they were with me the moment was influenced by my presence. The only way I could learn the truth was to ensure that they were more conscious of themselves than they were of me.

"I'm sorry to hear abour your mother," I said.

"Yes. It was sad."

"How will your father manage?"

"He wants me to stay."

"A difficult decision."

The girl smiled. "Yes. Isn't it? I suppose I'll have to send for my luggage. My clothes and things. Do you know that they buried all my mother's best clothes with her in the coffin? All she had. It was such a waste."

"You always do that?"

"I suppose so. And everything else is burned." She shrugged. "It's the custom here."

We were silent for a while. A scarlet float plane came over the tops of the trees and splashed down off shore and taxied in to the dock. It was the scheduled flight. The pilot jumped out and tied a rope to an iron ring. Four passengers climbed out and walked up the jetty. One of the passengers was a girl of about twenty; she wore a black silk dress but her feet were bare. Her naturally dark skin was burned almost black. She came up the path and grinned.

"Hi!"

I said. "You look terrible. What have you been doing?"

"I feel terrible. I've been berry picking down south. Got tired of it and hitched a few rides."

"Make any money?"

"No."

"What will you do now?"

"I don't know. Just hang around at home."

She walked on up the path, and I said goodbye to the girl from Vancouver and went on my way. Homalco was a village of problems, those of time and place and circumstance. There was little I could do to alleviate distress. Many of the difficulties the people faced were medical and educational. The young woman who waved from a doorway as I passed had three children, one of whom was always ill. She, herself, came from the north. She once told me that she lived forty miles by boat from the nearest hospital. The second child had been born during a storm while the boat was forced to take shelter in a lonely cove. Her husband had a violent temper and used to pick the children up by the feet and bang their heads against the deck. He had been killed in a fight.

Down by the water was a small green house in which a family waited. Wooden steps led up to the door. Inside, we sat around the kitchen table. The oldest daughter, who had been living on the mainland fifty miles away, had committed suicide, and her four children were in a foster home. Application had been made to the court to have the children made wards of the government, and the date of the hearing had been set. The dead girl's mother asked me if the children could be sent to Homalco. Was it not right that they should be with their family? Well, yes. It was right, but who had enough room for four children? One of the aunts said that she would take three of them. She had a house and lived alone. But she could not look after the baby. The young man who was lying on his back on a small bed said he did not think children should be brought up on an Indian reserve. Then he closed his eyes and said no more.

The court hearing was in ten days. It would cost the grandmother sixty dollars to fly down and a little less if she went by water taxi. There might be a fishing boat available. It was all very uncertain. We all knew that no one could get to the hearing and that the children would be made wards and that they might never be seen again. And the real reason for this was that there was not enough money in the family for a plane ticket and the houses were too small to absorb four extra children. No one knew why the girl had committed suicide. How were they to travel to the funeral?

The mother stood with her back to the room and pretended to wash dishes in a bowl which was filled with cold water. I looked across at Elizabeth, the second daughter, who was eighteen, and asked if she could represent the family at the funeral. Yes, she said. She would like to go but she had no money. I asked her if she could be ready in an hour. She could fly with me for the first fifty miles, and I would arrange for the rest of the journey. She said she would be ready. I went out into the sunlight and wondered if an unknown taxpayer in suburbia would be pleased or sorry if he knew how his month's contribution would be spent. Perhaps he would prefer to help buy a machine gun so that we could better guard our freedom and democracy. Or perhaps he would like to have a street lamp outside his house . . .

The man who waited for me by the water's edge was about thirty. I did not know him well. He was one of those unfortunate young men who did not have a home and spent his life in other people's houses. He was not strong. Two or three times a year he had a severe attack of asthma and it was necessary to fly him to hospital. He had an income from the Department of Indian Affairs of about fifty dollars a month.

"Oh," he said. "John, I was waiting for you. I have a paper here. Came in the mail. It's about my kids."

It was, indeed, about his kids. I remembered the young man's story. He had been married, and there were three children of the marriage. His wife had left him and the children had been placed in a foster home. Several months ago the children had been sent to visit their mother who was in the United States. Then, without very much warning, the wife had been granted a divorce and the custody of her children. The paper I now read was apparently an order by a United States Court concerning children who were still wards of the Court in Canada. The whole mess probably grew out of a distant judge's conclusion that the children's father, being an Indian, would probably accept the order. The father would not know how to contest it even if he heard about it, which was unlikely.

"What do you want to do?" I asked.

"What can I do?"

"Well, I doubt very much if the American court has any jurisdiction over your children. Did you want custody?"

"I don't want them to go to the States. Surely they are wards of the government here."

"That's right."

"Could you get me a lawyer?"

"Could you pay a lawyer?"

"On fifty a month?"

"Well . . . There will have to be an application by your wife to a court here. Or you can apply to the court for the return of your children. That's the first step. We can write to the States for a report on your wife's circumstances."

"Would you do that for me?"

"Yes."

"I don't know what to do. I had very little education. But don't I have some say if I want the kids to stay in Canada?"

"Yes. You have. It may take time, of course."

"Will you let me know?"

"Yes."

"I don't want to be a nuisance," he said.

"Will you be here for the next two weeks?"

"Where else would I go?"

"I'll be in touch."

"I don't want to be a nuisance," he said.


The house at the end of the village was almost worse than nothing. It had a broken door and one window in the back wall. The wooden floor was so rotten that damp earth was seeping up where people walked. Unlike some of the houses, this one was not built high off the ground; it smelled of dampness and decay. There was a round, rusty stove in one corner. A small girl and a dog sat side by side in front of the stove.

I could write some depressing things about that house and about the people who lived there. Yet, in some ways, the family had more satisfactions than they did frustrations. In the single main room there were two old beds and a table. There were no chairs. There was no piped water. There was no place to hang clothes or store food. There were no toys, but the little girl by the stove had a comic book in her lap. Her father was working in one of the camps at the head of the inlet, a remote place which was very cold in winter time but so hot in summer that each logger was supplied with a portable fire extinguisher. From time to time, the men flew home and spent their pay cheques in one of the island stores.

The men worked hard. When away from home, they lived in a special group of bunk houses provided for Indians. They might spend a month in a cold, windy valley before they came back in the red Beaver plane. Their lives were lived along the mountain shore. The moment they received their pay cheque they were virtually penniless, because they owed everything they earned. The practice of working to pay off last month's bills was universal and seemed to be accepted.

The little girl told me that her father was expected home in two days. He always stopped in at the store and bought her some candies. Her mother was in hospital. Someone had hit her on the head with a piece of wood. Oh, she was all right, but there had been blood all over the floor.

I left the house, and the sunshine outside was almost blinding in its clarity. It was pleasant to feel the heat on my shoulders and to see the mountains to the south fading into the blue sky and to hear the laughter of young people outside the church. It was difficult to realise that this was the place which had been snow covered, the paths sheathed in ice and half the village stricken with flu and pneumonia.

For two weeks no doctor or nurse had been able to reach the village. I had arrived on one grey day when every member of a family lay silent and ill on one large bed. You could feel the fever in the air like an electric charge. Four of the youngest children were in a heap under a blanket. One reached hospital a few hours later on the very edge of death. Fever and malnutrition had drawn the small body into a state of shock. The child survived. It was something of a miracle, but the hospital doctors still worried about the old people and the young children who lived on the far side of the wind, so to speak. By some freak of administrative genius, Homalco came under the Indian Superintendent in Vancouver, a hundred miles away. The village was the responsibility of the Health Nurses, who came from a small town forty miles to the south, and I lived fifty miles to the west. The various administrative officials never met one another. During the worst days of the flu epidemic I telephoned the Health Office and asked if a nurse could fly over to check on the situation. Well, a voice said, it might be possible, but it was difficult to ask a nurse to make such a flight in winter time. And this was true.

Luckily people soon forget about the winter when the clouds blow away across the mountain peaks, and the sea is calm and the fishing boats lie against the dock in the sunshine. I used to pass many happy hours in the homes at Homalco, and, if the time was wasted, nobody glanced at the clock as if they had a better way of spending the afternoon. In our individual and separate ways, we would be trying to disentangle the lines of communication. I was not really there at all, not as a person with memories of Paris and Lemnos and West Australia and the quiet, green mountains of Ceylon. I was some kind of inanimate, white faced switchboard. If the external struggles the people had with weather and bureaucracy and employers stopped for a while, then the internal struggles became obvious.

And so it was that six of us sat in a room with a window looking out across the water, and the tide seemed to rise almost to the front steps. The man sat at the table; he was a bit of a patriarch, Victorian in outlook and rather more than less an Indian. He had not been well enough to work for many years and had grown querulous and frustrated by years of arguing with Indian Affairs men, storekeepers and people like myself. Like many of the Homalco men, he wished to keep control of the family but was trapped by changing attitudes and situations. For instance, his wife could always find summer work in one of the island resorts where she would look after the laundry. The man had too much pride, if that is possible. In order to improve his position as head of the family he tried to give a demonstration of manipulation. He would tell me that he was sick and needed a plane to take him to town. I usually discovered that his power saw needed repairs. He took great care to miss the last flight home so that I would have to order a special plane. He would become stranded on a Friday night which meant that I paid for a hotel room in town.

All this was part of a game of chess. I did not mind losing face if it helped to preserve peace in the family, but, in fact, everyone knew what was happening and why it happened and the man's successful gambits impressed only himself. Behind his back, his wife made a face as if to say: Don't pay any attention to him. However, I was paid to pay attention to people and could not disengage whenever I felt like it.

Sometimes while people talked away about themselves I would be looking out of the window at the blue-green of the sea and the tide coming up over the rocks and the half circle of the village houses and there might be a girl in a Chinese coolie hat wandering along the path by the shore. A little boy sat naked in the dust.

The man was still talking, drawing my attention to the injustices of his world. He tried to use me as a club with which he could batter the storekeeper, which I did not mind, or attack the Department of Indian Affairs, which I did not mind, or assault my own outfit, which I did not mind. But I defended the airline which flew into the village in all weathers and the Indian Health Services who authorised and paid for the flights. I sometimes defended myself.

"Gibson. Would you talk to the storekeeper about my bill?"

"Yes," I said.

"It's six hundred dollars now."

"I know."

"Can you do something about it?"

"I'll talk to them."

"They charge too much."

"You're right."

"Would you fly down there now?"

"No," I said.

"You have something important to do?"

"I have to get back to town."

"It must be very important, what you have to do in town."

"Yes. I want to eat."

"Will you arrange a flight for my next doctor's appointment?"

"If you are ill," I said.

"Ill. I'm always ill. The doctor wants to see me."

"All right. And is the power saw working now?"

"No good. No good at all. I have to take it back for repairs."

"Oh," I said. "Well you won't need it until you feel better. That's something."

A girl was sitting on the steps of a blue house at the top of the village. She said: "Hi. My father's mad about his pension, you know."

"What's he mad about?"

"They cut him down because he owns a boat."

"Yes. I warned him that would happen."

"The boat isn't worth fifty cents," the girl said.

"Well, maybe not. But your father thinks it's worth a thousand dollars."

"Can't you talk to him?"

I said: "He's happier having an imaginary boat."

"O.K. Then tell the pension people it's an imaginary boat."

"I don't think they'd appreciate it."

"They ought to be more flexible," the girl said.

Village life is village life all over the world. You find the same feuds and jealousies and understandings and forgiveness. People are close to one another. If there is a funeral, you know who is being buried. If there is a fight you are interested enough to take sides. You are always involved. I may have been in the audience, but the drama was like a little whirlpool; it sucked in the stray passer-by. Homalco, like most Indian villages, was very preoccupied with its own destiny. Life revolved in endless circles. Sometimes, thought and action were no longer governed by intellect and reason; they were uncontrolled. At some point, I had to extricate myself and fly back to the town where I lived. And when, at length, I drove through the streets and stopped at traffic lights, the town appeared calm and orderly and completely lacking in spontaneity. Even my office, where telephones rang and typewriters rattled, seemed as peaceful as a monastery. And somebody said: "I don't know why you waste so much time with those Indians. You haven't completed the monthly statistics on your caseload."

# 9

# The Green Schoolhouse

IF you analyse the schoolhouse you end up with so many yards of concrete and a number of board feet of lumber, some nails, a little furniture, glass for the windows and the furnace. There are two classrooms on the main floor, each

containing desks and blackboards, blinds for the hot weather
and a picture of the Queen. There is a hallway where the
children can hang their coats and leave their shoes. The
teacher has a kitchen, a living-room, a bedroom and a
study. Behind the building, hidden by trees, is the electricity
plant.

That is the building. On most days of the year, two other
ingredients are added; the teacher and the students.

From the windows of the front classroom, you can see over
the village, over the rooftops to the grey-blue waters of the
strait. And in the distance there are mountains with snow
on the north side of the peaks even in mid-summer. From the
rear windows in the school, you see only the trunks of trees
and rising ground. In fact, the land behind the village rises
steeply to six thousand feet and is a place of rock and ice
and mist; it is the haunt of cougar and mountain goat.
There is no trail over the mountains.

The teachers come from all over the world, from England,
Denmark, Germany, the Philippines, from the United
States and Africa. They stay for one year. Each September,
a new face arrives on the scheduled flight from the town,
which is fifty miles away. The teacher will walk up to the
school, open the door and, very often, find that the basement
has flooded. There is no oil. There is no electric light. There
is no sign of school books or supplies. Probably, the first week
is the worst. Urgent messages are sent in by the pilot of the
plane, who knows exactly what to pass on to Vancouver. He
has seen the same thing happen every year.

It is really no easier for the students. Most of them have
been born on the reserve. Many of them speak their own
language at home. But they drift into school on the first
morning and sit at their desks and give the teacher their
names. This is the first difficulty, because James Peter is now
living with his mother but he calls himself James Joe when
he goes to live with his grandfather. If the teacher should be
so unlucky as to find last year's list of names, he will wonder
where James Joe is. The students will only shake their heads

and then look down at the floor. James Peter will wonder what all the fuss is about. When the monthly list of absentees is sent to Vancouver, James Joe will be included, and the number of absent students fluctuates until the teacher realises what has happened.

It is almost impossible to teach Indian children in the normal fashion. They do not like to discuss abstract things like democracy or the balance of power; they are not interested in the Roman Empire, because their culture developed without Greece and Rome and the French Revolution. They have no concept of discipline, but are about the most obedient children on the North American continent. They are brought up as individuals with obligations to the family. No one interferes with their private and personal lives. They are expected to follow the example of the parents and grandparents.

The village is isolated; it lies in a small cleft on the steep shore. An inlet runs for eighty miles into the mountains, where there are glaciers and peaks which are lost in clouds for much of the year. The swirl and turbulence of the winds along that shore deter even the most courageous pilot. The village is cut off from the rest of the world for two or three weeks at a time.

A few years ago, the airline installed a radio in the school so that help could be summoned in emergencies. One teacher, a man of sixty-six who had pretended to be younger in order to get the job, spent several days trying to make the radio work so that he could have a case of port sent over. From time to time, the people of the village would summon in a plane to remove a sick child. Very rarely, a nurse visited the place to examine the school children. Accidents were common. In one year, there were four drownings, one death by poison, one death by falling, one death by suffocation. In spite of a very efficient emergency plane service, babies died during flu epidemics and old people died because they were old and unattended.

Each teacher was responsible for first aid, and a cupboard

in the school should have been filled with drugs and bandages. The cupboard was usually empty. In any case, few of the teachers wanted the responsibility of patching up the men and women who turned up for treatment on a Saturday night.

If the village was isolated, the school was even more so. There was little social contact between the village and the teachers. There were problems of communication. Almost every teacher made the initial mistake of trying to solve social problems which, he thought, were ruining the children's education. There were, for instance, two women teachers who had been missionaries in Africa. They disliked the appearance of some of the children one morning and sent a very abrupt note to the mother. How could she send the girls and boys to school in that way? Had she no pride? She would have to do better or keep the children at home. It turned out that the mother was blind and was, in fact, performing a small miracle in getting her family to school at all.

A teacher would go down to one of the houses to find out why Alice was not at school. Alice said that her mother was sick and wanted her at home. The conversation would become an argument which was pointless, because neither side understood the fixity of their separate positions. The teacher was concerned that Alice go to school, partly because of the educational advantages and partly because of the law. It was decreed that children attend school until their sixteenth birthday. Parents who kept children out of school could be prosecuted. If the teacher was inexperienced, which was usually the case, he would start by appealing to the mother's sense of generosity and unselfishness. His voice would become like the note of a single wind instrument, not heard because of the height of the frequency. A dog whistle. A birdsong. And Alice's mother, propped up in front of the waterless sink, would be thinking of something quite different. Alice would be in the bedroom with the baby.

In the middle of this, Alice's father would arrive back from his boat which lay alongside the dock. He knew the teacher by sight and would smile and lower his head politely and sit down at the table, a man apart.

The teacher was really beaten from the start. He was the victim of the arbitrary decisions of demagogues who had assisted in one form of evolution. According to his thinking, Alice had to learn two or three books of potted knowledge every year until she was sixteen, preferably continuing until she was eighteen. At that time she would travel to another institution where she would continue to learn. Someone, long ago, had decided that certain books were needed for certain age groups. Someone had decided that when so many books had been read the education was complete. The child would become qualified to do certain jobs to earn a certain, specified income. This income would be used to live in a certain way, used to acquire certain well known possessions, used to support other children who would follow in the same path.

Neither Alice's mother nor father thought along these lines. Alice, herself, looked on school as a building in which she was confined for certain hours of the day except in the summer when she went out on the boat with her father. She had never been told to go to school and thought that the teacher was extraordinary, even rude. White people were very peculiar.

Alice's father wished that the teacher would go away. He had already decided that the teacher was a rude, interfering bore. There were so many other things to talk about. A killer whale had been sighted off the village. The plane was an hour late. A new logging camp was being established five miles down the coast. The roof of the house was leaking. The Chief Councillor had called a meeting that night to discuss ways of getting oil drums from the dock to the little building where the electricity was generated.

He said: "Killer whale off the dock this morning."

"Really," the teacher said. "That's interesting. D'you get many around here?"

"They come and go."

"Well. I came to find out why Alice can't attend school."

"Oh. She's helping her mother."

"The law says she must attend school."

"I don't know about that."

"Doesn't Alice want to go to school?"

"Plane's late," Alice's father said.

As the days passed, the teacher started to realise that there were more important things in the village than education and the school. The hours the boys and girls spent in the classroom depended entirely on the family circumstances and situation. Some had special reasons for being away; others had their own reasons for being present. The whole village was balanced so precariously between survival and disaster that learning was a form of leisure, having very little connection with the future.

For instance: few of the men earned more than $3500 a year. In order to buy food, it was necessary to go by boat to one of the small stores on nearby islands where prices were much higher than in towns. The stores offered credit which was paid off each month when possible. The men were always in debt. They worked to pay off last month's bill. When the logging camps closed, the men had to wait for six to eight weeks for their unemployment insurance. Sometimes the wife could find work in the store, or cleaning fish, or doing the laundry for tourists in one of the fishing resorts. When the wife worked, the oldest girl stayed home from school.

If the husband was away, the oldest boy took the boat to the store. If one of the small children was sick, the wife would fly over to see a doctor in the nearest town. She might be stranded away from home for two or three days because of bad weather. The cost of the flight was advanced by the store, or, in certain cases, was paid by the Indian Health Services.

There were months when firewood was short and the houses were cold. Boats went out to look for logs which might be afloat or stranded along the shores. There were days when the village was busy with its own affairs, days of funerals or weddings or of preparation for the boat journey to the fishing grounds. Sometimes, families travelled to other reserves to visit relatives. In summer, the children picked berries, which were canned for winter use. In other words, if there was nothing more important to do the children went to school.

Each year, the teacher tried to alter the social life of the village in the interests of education and each year there was a crisis. One Scandinavian teacher brought in the police because he wanted to prosecute parents of children who were away from school. He also thought that he could stop the drinking of home brew. Within a week, he had to leave the reserve and camped uncomfortably in a tent on a desolate part of the shore some miles away.

An Indian reserve is like any other community; it has a centre, a focal point. This point can change through the seasons. It can be the church; it can be the dock where the boats are tied up; it can be the schoolhouse. In isolated places, the teachers were the only outsiders who were capable of making an impact. Certainly, their remote presence made a difference to the community. But the schoolhouse itself was usually the most imposing building and often the only one with electric light. Thus, the basement was used for band meetings, concerts, the showing of films. Visiting civil servants stayed the night at the school. It is obvious that the personality and philosophies of the teacher radiated out into the homes and the hearts of the Indians. The effect could be good or bad, depending on the understanding, tolerance and experience of the outsider. Village tensions were very great. It was not unusual for a man to lose his job in mid-winter because of heavy snowfalls on the high ground where logging took place. If the mail plane was kept away by gales, all the normal processes of applying for unemployment insurance would fail. The computer in far off Vancouver would not have an answer. Equally, the grants paid under the welfare programme would be delayed. Civil servants in the city would send off a routine letter which would contain certain questions. They would then go home for the weekend. The letter would find its way to the airline office where it would sit in a blue bag until the wind dropped. Eventually, it would reach the reserve and be answered. The same thing could be repeated day after day. Meanwhile, the man would have to beg for more credit at the store. The family would be short of food. There was no soap for washing clothes. There was no money to bring the older children home for Christmas if they were away at residential school. And it did not take long to reach a flashpoint of frustrations and anger. If, at this point, the teacher sent a note to the mother in which he criticised the quality of the school lunches or the state of the children's clothes, the reaction might be unfortunate.

The Indians had a positive and cultivated disregard for the civilisations in which they were engulfed. Therefore, on the morning the teacher hoisted the maple leaf flag into the bright, September air, he was issuing a challenge. He did not know it at the time, but his challenge was always accepted. The ringing of the school bell was the opening shot in a war of nerves, of attrition. If the teacher survived the first year, he would develop an empathy with the people of the village. If he survived the second year, he would see the separate identities of each individual, the class structures, the feuds, the family solidarities and jealousies. He would feel the strength of the community, the steel blade of a culture normally hidden by mists of prejudice and prejudgment. If he survived the third year, he would begin to hate his own selfish society.

At night, and in the cold winters, the village lights would be the subdued glimmers of oil lamps. The windows would be half hidden by icicles. From higher ground, the brighter schoolhouse windows might seem to be symbols of knowledge and edification. But the process of educating the children in a minority community faltered and failed. It grew more hopeless as it advanced. Those students who passed the test in the village school were sent away to a residential institution which was administered by the religious denomination of the area. Reserves were normally classified as Catholic or United or Anglican or Salvation Army or Pentecostal. It was impossible for a Catholic to live on a Pentecostal reserve, mainly because there was only one church, one graveyard. Thus, students were segregated in two ways. If some went to town and lived in boarding homes, they often attended a parochial school and were thereby segregated again. Those who went to the Provincial schools were technically integrated, but this was only successful so far as the moralists were concerned.

The young Indians came from a society which was not competitive. Their I.Q.s were often above average, between 105 and 110. The hereditary factor was favourable, because the Indians, in their primitive state, had a high intellectual grasp on their own technology. They used their resources well. Probably, they were more efficient than modern, western society. They were very religious and had a complex metaphysical system. The Indian students had great potential. Unfortunately, this potential was not often realised.

Despite hysterical writing about reserve life, the years at home were not filled with deprivation. If there were differences in the treatment of children, it was not worse than elsewhere. Most of the environmental damage was done during the period of integration. Sometimes the language was strange. The attitude of white children was strange. Discrimination formed quickly; it was a mixture of economics, individual psychology and myth. The materialist society into which the Indian students had been plunged took note of the students' appearances. Poverty became appreciable. The reserves which were close to large towns were, of course, affected by social inheritance. But the students from isolated areas were the ones who suffered most. Their I.Q.s dropped an average of two points a year. Some, perhaps, had formed part of an aristocracy in their own community. In the outer world, they were forced by the attitude of society to meet only with the poor and the families whose children were intellectually handicapped.

It was not surprising that many young people left school and returned to the reserves. They had had enough. But their problems were not solved, because home life often seemed very different after four or five years in a city. The discipline was confusing. A girl of eighteen might be expected to help in the house almost to the point where the mother could retire. But other things, the personal existence which is so much the concern of white parents and foster parents, would never be mentioned.

In this situation, taking place in many families, the position of the teacher became important. He was a link between two worlds; he could, if he dared, offer advice and comfort. Young people came home because they were disenchanted or because they were homesick or simply because they were not understood by the people with whom they boarded. They had not lost faith in knowledge or education. Perhaps they realised that the full range of human ability was available to all races. What had gone wrong was that they were inevitably written off by a system which was unable to digest them. Society was imperfect; it could not or would not defeat racial problems by treating people as individuals.

The little stories of success and failure, intolerance and dedication, were taking place in every school which still survived on a reserve. There was a nun who drove twenty-five miles every day to open a kindergarten. She travelled in her small car in ice and snow, rain and wind, sun and dust. She never missed a day, five days a week, month after month and year after year. She taught slowly and carefully.

Each hour was a struggle, an attempt to communicate, to make the children speak to her. What did she think as she sat in the bleak schoolhouse and gazed at the faces before her?

There was a young couple who went out with their child to the remote places on the coast. They made the inevitable mistakes by intervening in family arguments, trying to change habits and customs and behaviour. The Indians cut off water to the school. The children failed to attend. But the young couple stayed on to make the school a successful and important part of village life.

There was a girl who taught for two years on a small island which could be isolated for weeks by winter gales.

One mad Englishman had electric organs and short-wave radio sets and all manner of equipment sent to the school. He taught the boys to play soccer and the girls to dance the tango. He was treated with affection by the students who recognised a kindred spirit. His progress was enthralling, and the Indians were so confused that they were unable to use their traditional methods of destruction. The Englishman never remained in one place for long; he completely disorganised the Federal accountants as far away as Ottawa. He had a happy disregard for the credit system, banks, finance companies, all forms of possessiveness and property. He departed like a shooting star which vanishes behind a church spire. You expect to see it again, but it does not appear. Somewhere in the darkness it has swung to a new course. Its parabolic orbit takes it out into unknown skies.

Not all the teachers, of course, passed through the scene with a flash of inspiring light. One who I remember, was a stiff, unbending and Victorian figure who started his reign on a particular reserve with the imposition of rules. He disliked isolation. He became silent and withdrawn, sometimes caustic. He demanded that all children under sixteen attend school or be taken away and charged with truancy. He wrote letters to the police and even mentioned the name of a young girl who was almost sixteen and was waiting to get married with the approval of her parents. In order to save the overworked policemen a long and fruitless boat trip, I took the girl away with me and found her a boarding home in town. She was to go to school, but her record showed that she would have to sit in a class with much younger girls and boys. It did not take long for the principal of the public school to explode. He took one look at the tall young woman who arrived smoking a cigarette and reached for his telephone. What did I think I was doing? Would I please remove the girl at once. Where did she come from? How did she get there?

Superimposed, so to speak, on the normal and classical dangers of movement to a strange culture, was the normal feeling of homesickness. Most Indian children who were transported to a city looked back with nostalgia to the little green schoolhouse. If such places had their limitations, they were better than many cement jungles in towns. The limitations were, in fact, part of the flexibility which gave strength. Poor attendance was better than no attendance. Boredom was better than hostility. A measure of indifference was better than destructive competition. The isolation of an entire village was better than the isolation of one child in a public school. Happiness was better than misery.

In a few years, the last school on a reserve will close. There will not be much left except some bright memories in the minds of grey-haired teachers, a few ruined buildings and some sodden exercise books thrown into dark corners by the messengers of progress.

# 10

# The Smoke Signals of Kyuquot

My supervisor had said: "We must stop all this colonial social work in the area." He was an ambitious young man who had arrived from the School of Social Work with a new degree. On his desk beside him, he kept his school notes. Each and every problem in our district of thirty thousand square miles was supposed to have its solution in the note books.

It was my day for visiting Kyuquot, a small settlement on the west coast of Vancouver Island, about an hour by plane across the mountains. The initial problem, therefore, was to travel from A to B, and by turning my head I could look out through my office window and make a preliminary judgment of the weather. It seemed to be a typical day of early spring with a light wind and high white clouds to the west. Fair enough. I put a call through to the airline. Departure time ten-thirty. The dispatcher said that we might have a difficulty on the coast because of fog on the shoreline. This was routine during the spring and summer, but there were always alternative places to visit. I pulled out my Kyuquot file and glanced through the letters which had come in since my last visit.

The settlement itself was at the mouth of one of the inlets which ran from the Pacific into the mountains. The harbour was formed by an island which curved like a turning shark close to the mainland. The eastern side of the island was well protected from winter gales. The two entrances were very narrow. During the fishing season, the place was crowded with boats which departed in the fall, leaving only the Indians and people like the storekeeper, the teachers and a few others to face the winter. There were two larger islands a mile to the west, and on one of these lived most of the men, women and children of the Kyuquot tribe. They remain today a prosperous, sophisticated and proud group. Their wealth comes from the sea. Kyuquot was the scene of the last great tribal war, but it is now a place of tranquillity.

There is no road to that part of the coast. People travel in float planes. Supplies come in by barge from Vancouver. To the south, there are miles of white beaches, deserted unless a deer or a seal pauses briefly at the water's edge. Sea lions lie on the rocks which form part of the coastal reef. You can see eagles and black bear and even wild cattle which are descended from domestic herds brought in by early settlers.

The psychological frontier was passed as we flew at eight thousand feet with a forty knot cross wind and a growing cloud cover between us and the land below. At thirty thousand feet the wind would be a full gale. But the lakes we could see were like glass. The valley trees were still, and a man looking up at us as we passed probably thought that our journey would be effortless. It was for me, of course. The pilot had to know in which direction to fly and how best to drop from the mountains to the sea. All the pilots with whom I flew were able to anticipate turbulence, and they would throttle down so that we were less shaken by the solidity of the air currents. We dropped towards the clouds which had grown more opaque as the minutes passed. It was sometimes possible to see the water of the inlets. Our route, that day, was due west to the Pacific shore. We came out over grey sea with surf over the reef and on beaches. The final waves broke against the shoreline.

This was the usual route. We turned north along the coast, flying half a mile off shore and sometimes isolated by banks of mist so that the warm little cabin was our special world and the drone of the engine so steady that it was unheard. We could smoke a final cigarette on those last miles to Kyuquot. We did not talk very much. The pilot might ask if I wanted to go out to the island, and he would shake his head as he looked down at the waves, not liking the idea of beaching the plane. I was not at all keen to go ashore in one of the dug out canoes the Indians sometimes provided. The canoes were unstable and had a low free-board. They were usually half filled with dirty water which slopped around and filled my shoes.

We decided to land in the more sheltered harbour where there was a dock and from which place I could travel by fishing boat to see the individuals and families listed on a piece of paper in my brown brief case.

"Down we go," the pilot said. The plane banked so that the floats seemed to brush the tops of the trees. Our arrival was precipitous. It was necessary to touch the water as quickly as possible, partly because of the small size of the harbour and partly because boats crossed from east to west continuously and they did not take much notice of descending aircraft. You had to land between boats.

The plane stopped bouncing. To our left, the main settlement was quiet, only a few fishing boats tied up along the docks. We could see the school, two stores, the house of the Fisheries Office, and the little wooden homes strung out along the footpath and protected by cedars. On an island to our right, the Outpost Hospital stood by itself and was made imposing by the flagpole on which flew the Canadian maple leaf flag. This was a Red Cross hospital, having a staff of one nurse; it could house four patients. Diagnoses and suggested treatments often came over the air from far away doctors by permission of the high frequency radio operators. Patients who did not respond to this kind of thing were flown to a Mission Hospital at Esperanza, and, if this did not provide the answer, the journey was continued to Vancouver. In very bad weather, when the planes were unable to fly, a motor vessel was used to move sick people to the nearest road connection from which point the ambulance could reach a hospital in an hour and a half.

However, small boats provided the transportation for most families on the coast. If you did not own a fishing boat, you travelled thirty miles or more to collect mail, buy food, visit the medical clinic, mainly in fourteen foot open boats which skimmed over the waves at high speed. The Indians thought little of spending four or five hours in overcrowded boats. They had no alternatives.

The seaplane dock at Kyuquot was in a corner behind the boats and close to one of the stores. We taxied alongside and tied up. Five or six people stood waiting, because our blue plane was easily recognised. I was reluctant to climb out, knowing that Caroline would have a long list of people who wanted to see me. I looked at my watch. The flight home would take an hour and fifteen minutes and grounding time was five o'clock. We would have to leave at half past three. Time was limited; its value had nothing to do with my pay but was concerned with priorities and weather conditions and the cost of the aircraft. I was easily the cheapest link in the chain.

Caroline said: "Mary wants to see you. George wants to see you. The teacher on the island wants to talk to you."

"How do you think . . . ?"

"Don't worry. I'll get Mary over."

Everyone had their own story about mysterious and unscientific communication between one native Indian and another. Some people I knew suspected a long range ESP system. Others had talked about a modern arrangement of smoke signals. The men and women of Kyuquot accepted the technology of the century and had developed their own communication network. Almost every house had a two-way radio with a radius of twenty-five miles. They could talk from the island to the reserve near the harbour, to boats at sea, to those who lived off the reserve near the store. Messages could pass down the coast from cabin to cabin and from boat to boat until it was impossible to escape from the net.

Caroline was a young Indian woman; she was married and had her own family. She was also my unofficial, self-appointed agent in the area. We walked over to her house.

While we drank coffee we could listen to the radio messages, for the set which hung from a nail on the wall was left switched on. When there was a silence, Caroline took down her radio and adjusted the antenna and spoke:

"Is Mary there? Is Mary there? This is Caroline."

"She's not here," a gruff, male voice answered.

"Do you know where she is? Over."

"She went over to the island."

"Over and out," Caroline said. She shifted the set. "I'll try and reach Veronica."

A woman's voice said: "Caroline. Mary is on George's boat. Has Gibson arrived?"

"Yes," Caroline said abruptly. "Ocean Spray. Ocean Spray. This is Caroline."

There was no answer for a moment. Then a voice said: "Caroline. This is Lucy. I'll try to reach George for you. O.K.?"

"O.K.," Caroline said. "Out."

The set was on the table. We could hear the subdued chatter of voices as we sipped our coffee and talked of other things. By that time an area of twenty-five hundred square miles was alerted to the fact that I was at Caroline's and would see Mary. The system was very public but no more so than any other way of sending messages in such a place. There were very few secrets in the Kyuquot Inlet.

I looked at my watch, but Caroline was not worried by time. She told me about her brother, who was missing days at school. Several months before, I had flown him to a town where he was supposed to benefit by a choice of schools, by integration, by a more sophisticated setting. But he had no idea of distances and had borrowed a bicycle and had been found many hours later, lost and unhappy. He was thirty miles from his foster home, still pedalling in the wrong direction. After three weeks, his homesickness was so acute that I had sent him back to his parents.

"He gets blamed for what other boys do," Caroline said.

"Not always, surely?"

"Most of the time."

"Does he never do anything wrong?"

"Yes. But he doesn't get caught."

"I think I'll go down to the school," I said.

"I'll let them know."

The walk to the school was along a trail between the trees. From the trail, you could see the horizon of the Pacific. Where there were patches of sunlight, the water was a bright blue. There were some fishing boats at anchor in the lagoon between the islands. While walking on the trail, I saw George's boat coming into the harbour, so I went down to the dock below the school and sat on an empty oil drum. The boat came alongside and Mary stepped ashore. She said:

"Long time no see."

"You are looking well."

"I'm getting married next week if the priest comes."

"That's good news."

Mary smiled. She was a pretty girl of seventeen. "Could you sign the papers for me?"

"No."

"My father and mother are both dead, you know."

"Yes. Well, there's a man in Victoria called the Official Guardian . . ."

"We're getting married on Monday."

"Definitely?"

"If the priest comes."

The people on the coast were always trying to keep up with the bureaucrats who had no representatives in the area. Girls tried to register babies and the forms vanished into the mysterious mists of the south. Medical cards were lost or the Federal department forgot to pay premiums. The Post Office tried to keep up with continual changes of address. Payments of Unemployment Insurance never arrived. The people were numbered endlessly; they had band numbers, social security numbers, medical numbers, welfare numbers, income tax codes, boat registrations. No one could keep up with the forms, even living in towns where there were large numbers of counsellors and consultants. Mary's predicament was typical. She had been born on one reserve but lived on another. Her band number was in an agency two hundred miles away. Her husband might belong to a band of the interior, and, when she married, Mary would use his number. Officials were kept away from Kyuquot by winter weather, by lack of time, by holiday schedules in summer. Anthropologists might arrive to ask Mary questions about kinship or her language. Economic advisers would pass through the area to assess the amount of timber ready for harvesting, the work force, the costs of transportation and so on. Fishing boats used Kyuquot as a summer base. Storekeepers came to make money. Priests baptised, married and buried. But, on the whole, Mary as an individual, seventeen-year-old girl was as unstudied and unknown as one of the small island deer.

While we talked, George came out of the wheelhouse. "Better get on board," he said. "I'll take you across the harbour. They want to see you over there."

There was a cool breeze on the water. Mary and I went into the wheelhouse and listened to the radio. George talked towards it out of the side of his mouth. I could not understand. Presently, he said:

"That was Caroline. She said you left your cigarettes behind."

The boat moved away from the dock, heading for the hospital. George put the boat on course and leaned against the forward end of the cabin. He asked if I would take his little boy with me. The child was losing weight. The doctor down at Esperanza was worried. Perhaps a larger hospital . . .

"You think he should go today?"

In a very short time, George was talking to Joseph, whose boat was at anchor in the lagoon. Joseph made contact with Veronica, who sent one of her children to see what George's wife was doing. While we waited for an answer, Caroline came on the air and asked me what I wanted done with my cigarettes. Before I could reply, Mary's sister was heard asking if Mary would please take home a bag of sugar.

"George. Do you receive me? This is Veronica."

"Go ahead. Loud and clear."

"Is Gibson coming to the island?"

George looked at me. I shook my head.

"No," George said. "Negative."

"This is Betty. Did Mary get the message about the sugar?"

"Get off the air," George said.

"This is Caroline. Gibson's pilot wants to know how long he'll be?"

"About an hour," I said to George. "Perhaps he can pick me up at the hospital."

"All right. You take my little boy next trip?"

"Next week. It might be better. I'll arrange a good home for him."

I looked back towards the dock near the store and could see the pilot walking along the path near the shore. He wore a light blue uniform, and you could see him quite clearly against the trees.

We were out of the shelter of the islands, and I realised how the strength of the wind had increased. The bow of the boat slapped into the waves. The red and white pennant on the mast shivered, and the halliards were blown out in a fine curve. George looked up at the sky, but he did not say anything. I looked up at the sky, because it was my road home. I knew how the steady, ocean winds became contorted and violent in the mountain passes. And among the tallest peaks, it was possible to see plumes of snow blowing off to the east.

"Caroline. Could you ask Gibson's pilot to pick him up at the hospital?"

"Roger."

"Send over his cigarettes."

"Roger Roger. I've a present for his old woman."

"Over and out." George turned to me. "Caroline has a present for your old woman."

"Yes. I heard."

Mary smiled at me and I said: "Don't forget the sugar."

"Oh, that. What am I going to buy it with? Peanuts?"

George had been listening to the radio. He said:

"Dick's wife wants to see you. He'll pick you up in his boat."

We reached the hospital dock and I walked up the grass path where the daffodils were shooting. There was a box near the path which was filled with glass floats. The Japanese floats were blue-green. There were orange-brown floats, which I was told were Russian. Some of the floats had come half way across the Pacific and had been washed up on the long stretches of sand between Kyuquot and Cape Flattery.

The nurse was waiting for me in the hospital office; she made coffee, and we sat and talked about Kyuquot and the Yukon and all the places she knew and loved. She had nursed Eskimo and Indian children and hoped to stay on the coast as long as her husband's job lasted. In my work, I had tried to be without prejudice, colourless, if you like. And sometimes I was faithless, because it was necessary to work with all religious denominations. The nurse at Kyuquot knew the Indians so well as people that she no longer thought of them as Indians. She had lived among them and accepted their ways of living and thinking.

The nurse looked through her notebook. She was slim and dark and boyish, not at all alarmed by her responsibilities. Could I arrange for a little boy with a cleft palate to go to Vancouver for examination, possible surgery and then speech therapy? Was it possible?

And one man had been flown out to the TB hospital and his wife and family had moved off the reserve and were unable to receive any financial help from the Indian Superintendent. I said I would help. In this way, we discussed all the notes in the small, black book and I made my own notes. After a while we finished our coffee and I went back to the dock. The plane had come to pick me up and Dick had arrived in a very small boat which was half filled with water.

"Almost time to leave," the pilot said.

"Well, I won't be long."

George was still there. He leaned out of the wheelhouse and shouted that Caroline wanted me to take a passenger back to Campbell River and that the teacher on the reserve was waiting to see me. Also there was a boat coming up from Nootka with a message that everyone in Nootka was without food. Could I fly down there on my way home?

By this time, the pilot was back in the plane with the door closed and his eyes closed. He was philosophical, because he knew that Kyuquot was only one small place in my twenty-nine thousand square miles of territory. If I left there on time I would probably be stranded somewhere else. What did it matter?

I sat in the bow of Dick's boat. When he jumped in the stern I was up in the air and as we bounced over the waves it looked as if the green water would flood right over the transom and fill the boat. But we reached the sheltered water safely. The tops of the cedar trees swayed and wind shadows crossed the harbour. Clouds came in fast from the Pacific, and it was cold.

Dick's wife had made tea. We sat in the living-room and looked out over the beach and under the long branches of the cedar trees. There were two or three islands to the west. Beyond them, the ocean moved sluggishly against the reef. The horizon was hidden by rain squalls. When we had finished our business, Dick said:

"I have a selection of words in our language you wanted. This was written by an American professor thirty years ago."

"Could I borrow it? I'll have a copy made."

"Would you like some more tea?"

"No thanks. I ought to go. The weather isn't too good."

"White people are governed by the clock."

"By the weather," I said. "Not by the clock."

"Next time you come you can talk Indian."

"But I already started to learn Tsimshian. You ought to have one language."

"We're all different," Dick said.

"Let's go."

We had an exciting voyage across the harbour in the skimmer. Dick was very nonchalant as we slid over the waves and ducked to avoid the spray. It took us about five minutes to reach the dock where the plane waited. The pilot was in the back seat. He woke up when we arrived and looked at me over his cheekbones. Then he climbed out and hunched his shoulders in the wind. He said:

"You're cutting it fine."

"I'm sorry."

"I don't think we'll get through the pass."

We stood by the plane for a moment. George and Mary walked down the dock and said that they would not fly in that kind of weather. Several messages had come through from Caroline. What did I want them to say to the Nootka boat? When would I be able to see the teacher? Could I bring some children's clothes? Lucy wanted me to take some baskets she had woven out of the local grasses. I might sell them for her. Someone wanted help in completing an income tax form. The storekeeper had asked if I would pay someone's bill. Someone's wife had been beaten. One of the girls was pregnant and wanted to talk about adoptions.

"Tell Caroline I'll be back next week."

"Right," George said.

I climbed into the plane. Ten minutes later we bounded into the air and rocked up over the tops of the trees and could see the open Pacific to the west with white water on the reefs.

"Busy day?" the pilot asked.

"Yes."

"I'll try and get some information about the pass."

The pilot called his base several times on the way home,

but there was no reply. In fact, his messages were not acknowledged until we were within four miles of the river where we landed, and by that time it was obvious that we would get home.

"I wish the Indians had radios like yours," I said.

"They know how to communicate, don't they?"

"Will you be flying tomorrow?"

"All day."

"Perhaps we could go to Nootka."

"Suits me."

When I reached home my wife told me that a message had come through by telephone from the Vancouver radio operator. It was from a man on Nootka Island, and the village was called Friendly Cove. There was no milk in the village for the babies. Could I do something quickly?

Even had one wanted to, it was impossible to fly at night in a float plane. By morning, there were low clouds and it was raining. A half gale blew from the south-east. It was four days before I was able to reach the coast again and drop from the sky into the little village of Friendly Cove.

## II

# Kingcome

IN summer time, Victoria is a white city suspended in the blue sea. The main highway to the north climbs over a mountain and follows the coast of Vancouver Island. You drive out on a brilliant morning and for five hours are never far from the eastern shoreline. The centre of the island is rugged, mountainous. There are no roads up the west coast.

It is about two hundred miles from Victoria to Kelsey Bay. The road ends; it simply peters out beyond the logging camp and the company town, beyond the harbour and the place where ferries load cars and passengers. If you want to go north from Kelsey Bay you have to take a boat or a float plane.

The water outside the harbour is known as the Johnstone Strait; it is a place of fierce tides, a slim neck of water reaching in from the Pacific, and it looks narrower than it is, because there are many islands. North of the open strait, between the islands and up great fjords, fishermen travel in summer and supply boats call in at logging camps. Tugs tow barges and log booms, sheltering in small bays during bad weather. North of the strait it is a masculine world except where the Indian villages survive. Not long ago, there were a dozen such settlements, but only half that number are now inhabited. People have left the more remote villages. Bands have amalgamated. Whole families have moved south to be near doctors, hospitals and schools. The old places rot. Tug crews, bored and destructive, set fire to those houses not pressed into the ground by snow and rain and gales.

There is a yellow plane tied up in the river at Kelsey Bay. Each morning it flies up the strait to Cormorant Island, which is now the main centre for Indian fishermen, the administrative base for the Federal Department of Indian Affairs, the Provincial Liquor Store and a small airline. The town is called Alert Bay.

If you are lucky, the yellow plane leaves on time and there may be a seat to spare. The pilot is probably European. He may have flown Danish jet fighters or he may be from Belgium or from England. His plane is a four-seater Cessna 180. You lock the car and walk down a wooden ramp to the edge of the river, which comes out of the mountains to the south, a swirl of snow water carrying branches and trees from the valleys to the strait. In the centre of the immense, remote and sun-washed scenery, the yellow plane is comforting and solid. The smell is petroleum, oil, cigarette smoke, hot metal.

Because it is possible to reach Cormorant Island without crossing a mountain, it is not necessary to gain height. The plane is pointed down river, into the summer wind. The pilot pushes forward the throttle, pulls up the water rudders and raises the flaps once the floats are off the water. It all looks very easy. Turn left. Fly at a hundred feet over the sea and the cormorant and the killer whales. Powder blue to the north with a snow capped Fuji type peak extending into the sky from a hidden range. The pilot lights his pipe. You may envy him on a calm day when the passengers are both happy and sober. It can be different. Haze may come down from Knight Inlet during a winter gale when the sky is dark and filled with rain and the strait is contorted and the only refuge is a swift river where gusts pass in different directions and with varying force.

It takes half an hour to fly to Alert Bay. The island is small, the town following the full length of the sickle shoreline which faces west. A hundred years ago it was an Indian village with totem poles along the sea's edge and tribal dances in the long houses and people sitting in the sun who could remember tribal wars. Now, the totem poles are in the graveyard and there is a large school, a hospital, a fish cannery, a residential school. Alert Bay has passed its peak; it survives because people live there. But prosperity is following roads, and the islands are unlucky.

If you want to go to Kingcome village you have to charter a plane. They will probably give you a two-seater Cessna 172, and the man in the airline office looks at his list of schedules. The office is a wooden building on stilts. From the window, it is possible to see the dock and the sky to the west. A red plane splashes down and taxis towards the north. It has UNITED CHURCH painted on its side in white letters. There may be a company plane, one carrying engine parts to a camp. The Royal Canadian Mounted Police have a blue and gold Beaver to supplement their boat service. And in the background is the wide strait with a hint of the Pacific horizon beyond the heat mist.

There is always movement. Alert Bay has two miles of road and seven taxis. People walk up and down the main street, looking in the store windows. Fishing boats arrive for fuel. And in the centre of the strait, freighters pass between hidden rocks.

There is no time to relax. Within half an hour you are sitting in the cabin of another plane, but this time the altimeter reads two thousand feet and the islands pass dreamily under the floats. Speed is one hundred and twenty. You are suspended over thousands of square miles of empty land. The mainland of British Columbia is a hundred miles away, but the coastal range of mountains looks close. The pilot says:

"Could be socked in at Kingcome."

"It looks clear ahead."

"Yes, it does. But there may be clouds down over the river. That's Kingcome for you."

"I know."

Not many people visit Kingcome village or have reason to be near to it. It is the only permanent settlement on five hundred miles of inhospitable coastline, and it is not even on the sea but several miles up the river. A boat would have to navigate its way towards the north, through innumerable islands, and the final thirty miles would be in Kingcome Inlet itself, which runs from west to east and then swings to the north at the last moment. Winds blow down the inlet during the four seasons. The winter gales are predictable. In summer, the heat of the interior will suddenly sweep down on unsuspecting fishermen, a wind that passes across ice fields and grows in strength as it enters the funnel of the salt water inlet. It is always possible to recognise the waters south of the Kingcome River, because the colour will be yellow, mud and clay from river banks brought down by melting snow. And the air will be turbulent. This was a little part of local knowledge shared by the pilots. It could be unpleasant knowledge. For one thing, no one likes landing a plane on a fast flowing river which is opaque so that it is not possible to see submerged trees. There is an element of luck.

At the top of the inlet you are approaching the mountains. The valley leads due north and the river comes from trees, diverted as it reaches the sea into a miniature delta. There is an area of swamp. Cottonwood and willow. No sign of life, only the yellow river winding up the valley with the encroaching mountains and rock peaks high in the clear blue sky.

The pilot is looking down, assessing the speed of the water and the direction of the wind. You are at five hundred feet, and suddenly the village appears below. A square tower of the church and buildings along the river bank and a Canadian flag flying and boats and men on the beach. There is a slight curve to the river. You circle three times, and everyone notes the position of the swirls of water indicating the presence of rocks or branches. Only the pilot has to think of everything at once and he decides to land upstream because there is little wind. He puts down the flaps, touches the throttle, swings the plane low over the trees and side slips towards the water. More power. You touch. A straight line across the river's curve and between the snags. For a moment, the plane sits like a sea bird in the middle of the stream and then moves up to the dock, which is on the right bank and across from the village. The passengers jump out and grab the wing struts and hold on until the plane is secured by a yellow nylon rope.

Two boats come over from the beach and ten minutes later you are in the village, in the warm, drowsy heat of the mountain summer. The houses are built on cedar poles. The river floods in spring time, and there is a water mark on each pole. Vegetation is luxurious, banks of elder, currant bushes, young pine and spruce and fir. There are two white fishing boats at anchor in the river. An old man sits outside his house, carving a mask from a block of wood. His wife is away, he says, ten miles up the river to catch fish.

There is no reason, in the modern idiom, for the village's existence. It was originally a place where people could survive. The salmon came into the river and the salmon, fresh or smoked, formed the basic diet. There were plenty of berries. There was fresh water. Two or three hundred people could avoid starvation, and that was their only real problem.

It is very quiet in Kingcome village on a summer afternoon. You are a hundred miles from the nearest car. There is no commercial logging nearby, but a man might use a power saw to cut firewood, the brief whine echoing across the valley. You can, of course, hear the children coming out of school. But the trees and the rocky cliffs behind the trees enclose you in a near soundless heat. Outside the church, little girls skip and jump around on one leg as little girls do anywhere in the world. Dogs lie in the shade. It is dark and comparatively cool in the houses. A woman sits in her kitchen and looks out at the river. Her baby is suspended from the rafters in a wooden hammock, strapped in securely like a giant chrysalis. A cord is tied to the hammock and to the woman's wrists, and the baby sways back and forth as if moved by the wind.

A somnolent atmosphere of seclusion and ennui. But it is impossible to forget the long, dark winter and the floods. Supplies come up from the south in a barge towed by a small tug. Oil drums have to be lifted out and brought up the river on the decks of fishing boats. Lumber for new houses, stoves, school equipment, all come the same way. Mail goes out by plane when the weather permits, but it is very common for the pilot to turn back. The engine of a Beaver can be stopped in mid air by violent turbulence. Or the valley can be filled with clouds so that it is impossible to see the river or the trees.

Kingcome village still lives, because the school is open and the church is used and because babies are born there. Young people marry and old people die. Moose are moving into the area from the north. Logging and mining companies inspect the valleys where flow the blue-white waters of the Atlatzi and Atwaykellesee Rivers. For the rest, the people prefer to sustain their own way of life. They are very conscious of the fact that they are members of the Kwakiutl ethnic group. They belong to the Tsawatainuk Band, of the Kawakewlth Agency, Indian Reserve Number 7. Even the baby in the hammock has a band number, but what use it will be to him in later years remains to be seen.

## 12

# Abel had a Daughter

IT all looked very simple on paper. Thesis: Social workers, church workers, men from the Company of Young Canadians, Indian Affairs Staff, School counsellors, nurses. Antithesis: Native Indians. Synthesis: Social progress.

Unfortunately, it was never like that. The Indians were not united; they did not agree with one another. The government officials rarely agreed with other groups. Everyone took up a very fixed position so that issues became confused and there was no true discussion. There was no real truth, or, at any rate, an attempt to find a real truth.

There were often moments during the day when one came across a high point of gaiety or a low point of sadness, and on such occasions it was possible to distil the whole range of human experience into a single, potent drop of meaning. Take the case of Abel. When I met him he was old, and he had lived all his life on a small reserve in one of the most barren and inhospitable parts of the coast. There were probably no more than eighty people in the community. The inlet was dark, and even the logging camps were established on floats which were tied to the shore and anchored with chains. In bad weather, the logs groaned and water slopped over the boxes of earth in which the wives tried to grow flowers. The houses creaked, and the children lived with orange life jackets tied around their shoulders.

The Indian village was on shore. Inland, the mountains rose steeply. The country was wild, grizzly country where it was necessary to have a rifle with you on a fishing expedition. There was a school. Supplies were collected by fishing boat when the weather permitted. The small boats met fierce seas, because that part of the coast was without the protection of outlying islands. Many people had died at sea. Many children were born on boats which had been forced to take shelter while heading for the hospital at Alert Bay. The people were used to hardship and they had retained their own way of life. They fished in the summer. They danced and sang at week-ends and were largely forgotten during the winter.

The isolation and impoverishment resulted in a certain aloofness, a feeling of superiority when it came to comparisons with the bands who lived near towns and had electricity, roads, cars and plumbing. The people of the inlet had to fight the elements and nature; they had to guard against in-breeding and ignorance; they had to retain warmth and affection in conditions which only encouraged bitterness and hate. And, as is so often the case, the more sophisticated Indians of the south were a little smug, even contemptuous.

I only visited the inlet twice, and each time the weather was bad. The pilot would try to hold the plane as it bounced up and down against the log float, and black waves came up from the open sea. Clouds would press down below the mountain tops and we would slide out into deep water and watch the wings brushing the tops of the waves. I was always pleased if the pilot was young and reckless and simply pointed the nose of the Cessna at the clouds. We would climb up into the mist between the mountains and eventually reach blue sky. This meant that we avoided a long flight down the inlet where we would be between the clouds and the waves and would spend an hour over the open Pacific. The only danger of flying above the clouds was that we might not find a way down and would become lost in the empty space. We have very few instruments, and as the floats touched the sea of white mist we never knew what lay below. It could be a valley, four thousand feet beneath us, or there could be a jagged mountain peak which we might see as a grey shadow, too close for comfort.

At least, we were warm up there and, if lucky, in radio contact with our base. But the people of the inlet had to travel in their small boats. When they returned home, it was to houses with earth floors, to a place battered by rain and wind. They had so little in that village that the accepted ethics and values of the West were unknown. The outer world might be better or worse, but it was the world of the future. From an administrative point of view it was easy to move a small village to a piece of Indian land on the north end of Vancouver Island. On paper, there were many advantages. The new houses would be more comfortable and would have electric light and telephones. There would be a road to the village, and the people could drive to health clinics, to public schools, to stores, to work. The experts had their differing opinions. Economists thought that the men would more easily find employment and that the work force in the new district would increase. Sociologists said that there would be many problems of integration but that it was better to plan a move than have it take place in a dis-organised way. Missionaries thought that the people would benefit materially but would lose their cultural identity and would drift away from their church.

Some white people were apprehensive about having eighty unknown Indians in the area and wondered if the school system could absorb and digest the children. Store-keepers were happy. The Indian Superintendent negotiated his way around the jungles of red tape, acquired land from another band, built the first house, dealt with public relations and all the other matters which became his responsibility.

The new village, when I first saw it, was a sea of brown mud in the centre of which were four department houses painted dark red. The fishing boats were in the river, some lying on their sides, some under water, some hauled out on to the bank. A week before, two children had died in one of the boats when the tide came in and flooded the boat through an open sea cock and drowned the little children while they slept. Already, although only a few houses had been completed, the people from the inlet were arriving daily. At one time there were three families in one of the new houses. Partitions had not been built, and the plywood panels were used as tables, beds and benches.

Abel was one of the first men to be given a house; he brought with him many of his relations, and there were about ten children under his roof. A fair haired girl was standing out in the rain; she turned out to be the public Health nurse who was working fourteen hours a day trying to solve medical and social problems. She told me that, as a result of conditions in the inlet, most of the children had lice, scabies and impetigo. One of the older girls was pregnant. There was no water piped to the house. There was no bedding. There did not seem to be any money to buy food. None of the children had gone to school. Abel was supposed to complete the construction of the house, but there were no tools.

It sounded very depressing, and the impression was not improved by the rain and the north wind and the mud which clung to my boots like clay. I can remember looking towards the town which lay two miles to the south, with the police office and the store and the beer parlour and those who were bigoted and many who were tolerant and I thought that it might take five years before Abel and his friends were settled. It might take ten years. It might never happen.

But there was no depression in the house where it was dry, and the electric light was reflected in the eyes of the man who smiled at me. We sat down side by side on a bed and talked about how much better things were in the new village. The smaller children were sleeping on the floor, little bundles of coats and shoes and black hair falling across their cheekbones. I was making notes of questions to ask the Indian Affairs men. The Superintendent was keeping away, not out of cruelty or indifference, but because he was wise.

In any case, he would be criticised. If he helped too much he would be called paternalistic. If he did not help quickly he would be called a bureaucrat. In fact, he was a benevolent man, looking rather like Inspector Maigret without his pipe.

Abel told me something about the life he had lived in the inlet to the north and about the boats that had been lost and the tensions during the long winter; he was glad to get away from a place of sour memories. At last there was something to look forward to. It would be a better life for the children.

Abruptly, Abel asked me if I could find his daughter.

"Where is she? Don't you know?"

"The missionaries took her away when she was six. The Adventists."

"Why?"

"They said she would have better education."

"How long ago was this?"

"Five years. She must be eleven now."

"Didn't you ever hear from them?"

"No. But I think they took her to Powell River."

I asked Abel for the girl's birthday and Christian names. For several weeks after that I tried to trace the girl, but there was a blanket of secrecy. Most people were incurious or they thought that the girl would be better off where she was. She would not remember her father. Why rock the boat?

The couple who had taken the child had moved to Vancouver and from there to the United States, and there the road ended. During the next two years, Abel often asked me about his daughter. So far as he was concerned, she was still part of the family.

Long before the last house was completed, all the people from the inlet had moved south. The impact of their presence was inevitable. Complaints were received from the school that the children were late in the morning. Some of them could not speak English. They had no books. They had not brought their school records. The nurse complained that there were no health records. What about immunisation? The store granted the people credit and then reported that no bills were paid. There were the usual Saturday night problems in the beer parlour when the Dionysian bliss could change, in a second, into feelings of outrage and hostility. Most of the people who lived in the town had come from the cities to the south; they were there to make money. They worked hard, and the conditions were comparatively poor. They were puritan, not understanding the Indian priorities. Only those who had seen life in the isolated reserves to the north could understand the attraction of being driven to town in a heated taxi or of being able to buy enough food for a week. How many could understand that it was a novelty to take a sick child to a doctor?

The transplant of a community does not always lead to rejection, but the solution to the problem of isolation is not simple. People become irrational and emotional, and there is always friction at the points of contact. One church group threatened a social worker with court action if any of the Indian children died. The alternative, they said, was for all the children to be taken away and boarded in the homes of white people. I used to think of Abel's daughter. Somewhere in the United States she was probably being taken to church every Sunday and learning to be a good Christian.

## *13*

# Death of a Village

WHEN I first went to the island it was winter time and three boats were tied up at the dock. One of the boats was an old seiner, and several mule deer were hanging by their feet from the boat's derrick, waiting to be skinned and butchered. A strong wind blew in from the Pacific. The water around the island was sheltered; it was calm, but gusts crossed the surface like cloud shadows. The tops of the trees swayed. Snow was falling on the mountains to the north.

There was a path through the trees to the village. The first building you came to was the school. It had been closed for two years. The windows were boarded. A ship's bell hung outside with a broken board below which said that the bell had been presented to the village school by someone. The school windows looked out over a small cove. There was a path along the shore, and the ten houses were spaced along the path. In the middle of the village was all that was left of an Indian long house, four corner posts carved with the head of Thunderbirds and sixty-foot logs which had been placed at the levels of the eaves and the peak. There was no roof. It was just the skeleton of a building, and the few totem poles left were either leaning over at an angle of forty-five degrees or were lying in the wet grass.

There were two fairly new houses in the village, but the rest were old and made of thin boards nailed on the frames. Many of the windows were broken. In such houses it was difficult to keep warm in winter, and the men spent a lot of time towing logs to the beach where the logs were cut up with power saws.

The people who lived there were irreverent, ebullient and independent. They lived from day to day, and one of the men told me that he would rather starve than ask the Indian Superintendent for help. In order to survive, he hunted, dug clams which he sold in sacks, worked in logging camps when he could and sent his sons up to Rivers Inlet in the little green boat which he owned. This spirit of independence was one which was encouraged when families started to rely on financial support from the government. But the same spirit was disliked by policemen and teachers and other officials. The young boys of the village were often in trouble, mainly because they did not give a damn for anyone. I found them quiet and pleasant and polite, always willing to discuss last year's fishing season and their plans for the next year. But when they took their boat across the water to Alert Bay, their arrival was noted by the police, whose idea of justice was that the community had to be protected. When an offence was committed, the sentence in magistrate's court usually had some kind of a geographical solution. Bad boys should be sent somewhere. This attitude prevailed in nearly all the small towns. As a result, we operated what was essentially an exchange programme. A bad boy from town A was sent to town B and vice versa. In my position as probation officer, I was supposed to report to the court from time to time, but it was very difficult to keep track of the boys. They did not accept the justice they had experienced and sat through the court hearings with a look of deep boredom on their faces. Sometimes they were ordered to stay at home, not to leave the island on which they lived. If I met them far away on the fringe of the city, they were not abashed. In course of time, the whole business was forgotten.

The people were leaving the island, and almost every month another house was empty, its windows boarded and the unmistakable appearance of neglect creeping over the walls. No smoke came from the chimneys. No washing hung on the line. It only took one gale and a leaking roof to end the house for ever. The rain in that area was heavy, and once the walls and floors were sodden there was nothing to be done.

The young women were the first to go. They did not make any important and final decision that on a certain day they would pack and depart. Rather, they simply did not return from one of their frequent journeys to Alert Bay or Campbell River or Vancouver. Many of them had aunts or uncles or cousins living elsewhere. Some married. Some became the victims of life in the larger cities. Their departure from the island obviously led to soul-searching by the men, but a move was easier for a girl. The men stayed with their boats; they stayed where they did not have to pay rent or worry about monthly bills for electricity and fuel oil. When, as sometimes happened, a whole family moved to one of the larger towns, their days became filled with worry and insecurity. They were entirely dependent on the routine cheque from a welfare office, and if the computer made a mistake, the whole world collapsed.

Once the people started to go, those left behind were unsettled and disconsolate. Old people did not want to leave. Some younger men took the whole thing as a challenge to their integrity as Indians and to their capability of surviving. But there was a psychological change. The peace of a hundred years became something which was almost hostility. There was more drinking. There were more fights. The survivors clung on with determination. And I walked in the cold wind with the boarded or empty windows on all sides and closed doors and silence. No one came out to talk about the weather or offer a cup of coffee. Even the children were invisible. Once, the village had been filled with dogs. I did not see one. The Thunderbirds looked at me with blind eyes.

I could see smoke coming from a chimney at the far end of the village and I walked down the grass path and went over to the house and knocked on the door. The man who let me in had been sitting in the half light. His son squatted near the stove, carving a little totem pole out of yellow cedar. Although the house had two rooms, all possessions were in the warm living room. The rest of the house was practically open to the wind. Even where we sat, sheets of cardboard had been nailed to the walls. There was a board across one window pane. The fire smoked. Crammed into the space were two beds, a pile of firewood, the skins of small animals hanging from a string, an old rifle, two oil lamps, faded photographs, a table covered with wood shavings.

The man's name was Sam and he was a widower. He once told me that his wife had gone off in a boat one winter day to do some shopping. There had been fifteen people on the boat, most of them women and children. Nothing had been seen or heard of them from that day. No wreckage or bodies had been washed up. The boat and the people vanished into the distance and probably were unwatched as they disappeared around the corner of the island. No one would turn their head on such occasions. "No sign of them," Sam said. "Strong tide here. Very strong tide."

He had brought up three sons there and, when he could no longer work, was sent fifty-one dollars a month by the Federal authorities. Somehow, they all survived. There were fish around the island and berries in the woods. Deer were plentiful.

Sam had sent out a message which asked me to visit him as soon as possible. It had taken me a month to reach the village, because the weather had been unusually bad. The winds had been strong, and I had twice flown over the area without being able to land. Now, we sat in the twilight of his bleak home and talked about the boys. It was one of the delights of my work, to travel through the winter skies at great expense to the government and the taxpayer. It was not the actual flying that was satisfying, but the fact that an old man could summon me from my warm office and know that I would arrive. For too long, in fact, Indian parents had been almost powerless to help their children. The generation gap on the reserves was a great fissure, a parting of minds that tore the nerves and tissues and blood; it was always changing in depth and width, like those sinister cracks in the surface of the ground during an earthquake. Even if Sam was half forgotten on an island which was a speck on the chart, he could send for me or someone like me. He could promise his boys that much. The very fact that I arrived was the important thing.

The boy had not really looked at me; he went on chipping at his totem pole, and the shavings were blown along by the wind which came like a knife blade through the crack under the door.

I asked what I could do. Sam was sitting, leaning forward with his hands clasped between his knees. He stared at the floor, and the silence was extended beyond the normal limit of my understanding. Had I been with white people, I would have repeated the question. As it was, I tried to think of something else. How would I take off in the Cessna with a narrow gap between the islands and a cross wind . . . ?

Sam said something in his own language, and the boy looked at me as if he had just been made aware of my presence. A gust of wind shook the house. Brown paper patches fluttered on the walls, and we heard the rain against window panes. A poor day to fly.

"You like flying?" the boy asked.

"Not in this weather."

"It's quick."

"Yes."

"I was wondering if you could find somewhere for me to stay."

"I expect so."

"There's nothing here," Sam said.

"How old are you?" I asked the boy.

"Seventeen."

"Where did you want to go?"

"I don't mind."

I was trying to remember exactly what infringement of the law had brought this young boy into court, how long his probation period had to run and what his life had been until that moment. Also, it was unpleasant to face once again the inevitable choice. There was nothing for youth on that particular reserve or in that particular village, but what was there for him in a strange foster home in an alien town? He knew who he was in his own home; he knew both his friends and his enemies. The language was familiar. And, in fact, there was a great deal to do. He was strong and healthy; he cut wood for his father, picked berries, helped the fisher-men clean their nets, boarded the broken windows, went away to do the shopping, fished for cod in his skiff, crewed on a seiner, cooked most of the meals and mended his own clothes. It was not a life of inactivity.

"Why do you want to leave?"

"Too much trouble here," Sam said.

"Oh, I see."

The boy was looking at me again. We understood each other, because an indication of trouble meant anything from village feuds to police investigations or shortage of money. Trouble meant that the equilibrium of life was threatened from inside or from outside; it was a word to describe the pessimism of those who had never experienced fair justice, had never even experienced good luck. Fate was on the side of the devil.

I said: "It would help if you had a relative you could stay with."

"I have an uncle in Alert Bay."

"Not Alert Bay."

"Why not?"

"You know why not."

The boy started to laugh. "I have another uncle in Sullivan Bay."

"Would you like me to go and see him?"

"Yes."

"Today or tomorrow, then. I'll let you know."

"That's fine," Sam said.

We walked together through the village in the wind, and I could see moss and grass growing on the broken tops of the totem poles. And as we reached the dock I looked back and realised that there was no church there, no school, no store. There was little to hold the place together. It would not be long before another enclave of native Indian life was abandoned to the rain forest.

On the following day, I flew the boy up to his uncle's house, which was on another island about eighty miles to the west. Only two families lived there, and there was no dock, only a line of logs running out from the beach with a dug-out canoe tied up against the last log. The boy was happy to try the canoe, which I had thought to be purely decorative or some sort of affectation like wearing moccasins. The boat was unstable, which meant that it was not possible to lean over, light a cigarette or even to sneeze. The boy paddled. I sat in the stern and wondered if the water was cold. When, eventually, we reached the shore, the uncle and aunt came to the door of their house. The old man apologised for the canoe; he said that it only capsized if the people in it were in too much of a hurry and that served them right.

I went into the house, but the boy stayed outside with a large dog, which he started to chase along the beach. Everything that happened was accepted as if the unexpected was really a matter of history and the future as clear as the past. No one asked me why the boy had arrived and he, himself, did not even question the fact that he was welcome there. I did not bother to explain, but said that I would send a little money each month for the boy's board and I would be disappointed if he went to Alert Bay.

I paddled myself back to the plane, and, once the canoe was tied up, stood on the float and looked back towards the shore. The uncle and aunt had returned to the house. The boy was sitting on a rock, and the dog sat beside him. I raised my arm in salute, but the boy did not move. We saw him still sitting there as we circled overhead at five hundred feet. He did not look up, but was throwing stones into the water. We could see the ripples spreading out to form a pattern on the calm, green surface of the bay.

I returned to Sam's island village on a blue summer's day when the air was still and the water between the rocky shores like thin milk. The sun burned down. The place was greener, more secluded. It was unusually quiet. Even the dogs were not waiting for me on the path. The village seemed deserted, and I walked between the houses, down to the beach and back to the edge of the forest. There was no urgency, no hurry to return to the plane. The pilot was probably asleep in the back seat with his feet propped up on the controls. So I lay down on the grass and tried to imagine what it would be like to live in that place. To my right, there was an old tree stump which had been carved in the shape of a wolf. Beyond, there was an open space covered with brambles. The old long house had gone. After many years, the Thunderbirds had refused any longer to support the giant logs; they had turned to dust. There was nothing left but a mass of soft, broken cedar with a wooden beak sticking out of the grass like a shark's fin. When I turned my head, the wolf was still there, staring at the ground, teeth bared; it gave the impression of being trapped on its rotting tree, carved fifty years ago but still very much alive.

This was a fishermen's village; it had many counterparts in other countries and on other shores. Life was simple and governed by such things as seasons and tides, wind, fog and moonrise. The boats were old or small or both. Each man's income was limited and had to spread over winter months. There were years when few fish were caught. Boats were lost by storm and fire. Life was hard, unrewarding from a material point of view. However, the people had been satisfied. In the context of native life, they had been privileged, progressive and contented. And as I lay on the grass and looked up at the blue sky it was possible to appreciate the normality of peasant thought and action. It was not very extraordinary.

I stood up and prepared to leave. And as I turned towards the path I saw an old woman outside one of the houses; she had crutches under her arms and leaned on them as she watched me approach. She smiled and nodded, and I asked her where the people were. She spoke little English but was able to tell me that the fishermen were in Rivers Inlet and that all the women and children and some of the older men had gone up Knight Inlet for a two-day expedition. They had gone to their traditional camping grounds.

I asked whether she was all right by herself. She said that she was safe. Her granddaughter would be home from Port Hardy before sunset. As we talked, humming birds darted over our heads and the sound of bees in the wild flowers was a steady murmur and the heat struck us with the intensity of noon. After the abrupt echo of our voices, there was silence. I had a sudden terror that I was in another place, in another land. For a brief moment, I seemed to emerge from a dream so that the village shivered in the haze and the deserted hills were covered with olive trees and I was on a Greek island, in an ancient world beside the violet sea.

Through all the days of the year, by flying through a thousand miles of sky, driving, walking, arguing, promising and writing, it was possible to postpone happenings, both the good and the bad. Sam's boys moved from island to island, from one foster home to another. If there was trouble, we talked to the police and made promises. We used up many gallons of high octane gas, hours of time, lots of forms and sheets of paper. And each year, the village became more empty and the boys less secure. Human behaviour was unpredictable, but we knew that it was affected by change and we knew that when a village died and the young people moved away they would alter their way of life. They would think differently and act differently. When the boys came face to face with discrimination and prejudice and injustice they struck back. It was a choice between imperilled isolation and ethnic suicide, often between boredom and gaol.

The last time I visited the village was in the fall. The sun was bright, but a cool wind blew from the north and the shadows of the trees moved restlessly on the path and the smoke from a chimney poured like water off a roof. The tall, dying weeds dropped their seeds on our shoes.

Three of us wandered past the empty houses that day. Gordy was our pilot, and the slim girl with fair hair had come to see the boys. She was now responsible for the well-being of many young people in that wild, little known area. She succeeded, as indeed we all should or would, by being scrupulously honest; she had not learned that other truth, the bureaucratic truth which, in the end, becomes fixed in so many minds as the ultimate good. In the course of time, legislation and regulation become more important than ethics, and at that point we are lost. We can no longer accept the realities of life as they confront us from day to day.

The boys were at home. One said that the police were looking for him. When he was released from gaol he would like to take a course of some sort. Was this possible? The girl looked at him for a moment. Perhaps there were many things she should say. She might talk about free legal aid, about the possibility of probation, about charges and evidence and witnesses. In the end, she answered the question; she said: "Yes."

There was little point in remaining there that day. I felt miserable and depressed. Month by month, the focus of our work changed. As people from the cities moved north and hotels were built and roads penetrated the forest, we were faced with demands from those who expected immediate service. A doctor thought that we should visit his clinic every month to explain the new medical plan and see that patients paid their bills. School teachers wanted to discuss children. A local man who thought he was important, and he probably was locally, complained that he had inquired about adoptions and had waited a week for a visit. A village clerk wrote a letter to the Parliament Buildings if one of us did not answer a letter within twenty-four hours. Politicians were worried about votes. Priorities altered. We were asked to spend less money on plane flights. As a result of all this, Sam and his sons were virtually abandoned, and the remorseless pressures began. Very few people would notice that one young man had been taken from an almost deserted village somewhere between the open Pacific and the coastal mountains. The young man, himself, would not protest. He had not expected much more from life in any case.

The scene was very beautiful on that cool, blue day

between summer and winter. We all walked back to the plane in silence. I do not know what Gordy was thinking about. The girl and I shared the knowledge of defeat. Possibly we were in the wrong place at the wrong time. Experts from museums could arrive to repair or remove totem poles. Linguists came and went. Forestry men arrived to look at the trees. Land speculators floated past on their comfortable boats. Only the human element was valueless. Whatever that might mean in the future, we were the only people who knew or cared about it at the time.

## *14*

# Friendly Cove

THE Spaniards called it San Lorenzo de Nutka. Captain Cook called it Nootka Sound. On navigational charts, it is Friendly Cove. The real name is Youkwat, and it is the home of the Mo-achat Indian tribe.

When, late in the eighteenth century, sailing vessels began to arrive from Europe, they required a refuge between San Francisco and the northern Pacific. Nootka Sound was suitable, because it provided shelter from westerly gales and there were safe anchorages in twenty fathoms of water. For many years, Nootka supplied the coast with interesting but fleeting foreign visitors; it provided the historians with a few pages in their books. But it remained isolated. No road penetrates to the southern end of the island today. In fact, the Indian village is almost deserted. The ruins of a fish cannery are being covered by the forest. The same prevailing wind that brought the Spanish ships to Nootka in 1789 now blows through broken windows and over the sagging rafters of old buildings.

I used to fly into Friendly Cove in a Cessna 180 fitted with floats, and, if it was rough off the shore, we landed on a narrow, dog-leg of a lake and walked half a mile along the beach to the village. Because much had been written about Nootka Island, by early explorers, missionaries, English sailors held prisoner by the Indians, anthropologists and historians, there was an opportunity to use imagination there, to visualise the Spanish fort and the square riggers floating out beyond Maquinna Point.

But history is one thing. Life is something else. The great days of Nootka ended before the Second World War, during the depression. There is a lighthouse there now and a small group of Indian houses on a spit of land which curves away from the Pacific and encloses the cove. You can find black jade on the beach; you can watch eagles fly down to the cedar trees and see deer on the trails. There are only a few boats now, and the plane comes down to a scene of quiescent beauty.

I suppose that Benedict was an old man, but he was active and independent. He had a small fishing boat and lived in the only surviving house near the ruined cannery. He had once been chief of an Indian tribe, but chose not to live on a reserve. So he made a home for his wife and family out of what had been abandoned by white men. No one could really complain.

It was a perfect refuge. Where the forest ended, there was a rock island, and the green, translucent water was always calm there. The water was deep right up to the shore, and Benedict could run the boat on to a strip of sand between the island and the coast of Nootka. The cedars encircled the bay. The cannery had been built out from the shore on wooden piles. There was still a wharf there, but the rest of the place was a mass of boards and posts and doors and window frames. You could walk in the roofless sheds and stumble over rusty stock anchors. Buildings had fallen into the water to be broken up by winter gales and swept away on the tide.

Benedict had found a house with a roof. He had put glass in the windows and had brought a stove up from the mainland. He was quite comfortable and was back in his own country. He had outlasted the industry and enterprise of white society. He told me that the great metal tanks which stood on the edge of the trees were still filled with fish oil that had become solid over the years. Forty years before, two hundred men had lived and worked there. I used to sit in the sun and half close my eyes so that the buildings looked solid and permanent, and it was possible to imagine all the activity which took place before the herring moved away and before the place died.

Benedict was not conscious of the cannery ruins but he pointed to the forest where the old mission church still stood and where there were a few little houses built by priests and Indians in the nineteenth century. Only a few hundred yards to the north, and at the head of the bay, there was a beach from which had been launched the first square-rigged ship to be built on the Pacific coast. But as my little blue plane rocked gently at the wooden dock, I talked with Benedict and his family about the present and the future. Because of the high cost of flying and the lack of boats, Nootka was now more isolated than it had been fifty years ago. Or it seemed that way.

The fishing boat was painted white but it was patched with a green scum as if it had lain under water for a long time. The engine worked, and the family thought nothing of heading up the inlet. After a six hour voyage they would reach a reserve where they had friends and could stay for a day or two. There was a road up to the town of Gold River, and there were stores in the town where it was possible to buy food and clothes. In bad weather, boats would be stranded at the head of the inlet for weeks at a time. Winds would come through the mountains from the east, gusting from valleys and bringing snow, which would blow horizontally away towards the open sea. Sometimes the water in the inlet was a seething mass of white waves when the flood tide met the wind, and no boat would venture far.

Indian children were brought up on the water; they had

no fear. I knew one boy who voyaged twenty miles down the coast in a small dug-out because he had a disagreement with his grandfather. And a girl of seventeen brought the family fishing boat a hundred and fifty miles from Rivers Inlet to her home village after her father became ill. Some Nootka families went forty miles to buy stores in fourteen-foot boats with outboard engines. They had to use the tides and they knew the meaning of every cloud formation and every change of wind. They were natural sailors.

Benedict lived for two months in the old house north of Friendly Cove. And then one day I heard that his home had been destroyed by fire. He had lost everything. There was no way to reach him by telephone or radio. The message had come to me in the early morning from a passing fishing boat, relayed from wavelength to wavelength and finally arriving by telephone at my house. "Benedict burned out. Please send clothes."

I flew over the same day and stood by the rectangle of black ashes from which smoke rose. The new stove had melted. The acrid smell of burned wood and clothes and rubber was in the air, and heat rose shimmering from the ground. Benedict was very practical; he almost ignored the ashes of his possessions and began to explore the surroundings to see if there was another building suitable for occupation. The children sat on the edge of the dock and looked down at the water.

The family, of course, knew the coast well. The loss of a house was not the end of everything. Benedict had been away for several years, and his children had been educated in the city. Now, they had rediscovered the land, which they felt was theirs. Away from the smoke, you could smell the sweetness of the cedars, all the strong summer scents which almost soothed like barbiturates in the long, warm nights when the sea glittered from moonlight or phosphorescence. And there were many places a family could use for a home.

We climbed away from the sea, following a path which led

through ferns and saplings alongside the rotted wooden pipe which had once supplied the cannery with fresh water. At the head of the bay there was a stone beach. Above, stood the old church. We explored the houses first, forcing our way through undergrowth to the front door of what may have been the priest's residence. The rooms were cool, shaded by trees so that to be inside was like standing in an undersea grotto. There was no glass in the windows. Part of the roof sagged down. There was a bath tub in a back room. But thirty years of snow and wind and sun had rotted the floor and made the house into a haven for spiders, mice and all the insect life of Nootka. The kitchen was filled with junk, pots and pans, bits of iron beds, an old wood stove, sodden books and the débris of an abandoned home.

Benedict suggested that we have a look at the church. Possibly he could write to the nearest priest and ask if the family could live there for a while. Possibly it could be deconsecrated by some backward motion of the hands. I thought that the ancient law of sanctuary could be used to protect a family, not from the abuse and violence of bigots and murderers, but from the heat of the sun and the winter cold. Sanctuary. It sounded very strange, and I wondered if anyone had used the word on the island of Nootka. Perhaps the captain of one of the Spanish ships . . .

The church had been well built, and, because the roof had survived, the walls and floor were clean and solid. Our voices echoed up to the little wooden bell tower. We decided that the main part of the church could be divided into four rooms, but the walls would not reach the ceiling. The windows would be boarded up except for those needed in the main room. We had to think of winter, of the months when the gales blew from the west. I did not know if the floor would keep out the cold. On that day, it was almost more pleasant in the church than out in the sultry heat of the forest. When we moved outside, we could see strips of bright, blue sea through the cedars and the whiteness of the ruined warehouses out on the island.

On the way back to the shore, we stopped for a moment to look down at the shallow green water. The tide was coming in. The bay was on the eastern side of the island, and the open Pacific was across the wooded hills. Thus, the water was calm, moving like clear syrup around the rocks and piles and along the edge of the beach. I could see the two girls down there, each with a bright red shirt; I asked Benedict if he thought that they were happy to be back from the city. He hesitated for a moment, because my question was almost too personal. Normally, he would have said: "Yes." The conversation would have ended. But he looked thoughtfully at the ground and lifted his shoulders. "I think so. I hope so."

"The church will be gloomy in winter."

"Yes," he said.

"Perhaps there's another house."

"Nothing with a roof."

But he was wrong. Lying in the sheltered water between the island and the beach was a float house. It was about forty feet long. Giant logs had been chained together to provide the foundation and to ensure buoyancy. The actual house, from where we stood on the high ground, was nothing more than a red roof, but the roof was intact. Benedict and I must have noticed the float house at the same instant, because we turned, without speaking, and went on our way down the path towards the beach.

During the next hour, we collected logs and planks and made a temporary bridge from the rocks to the float. Benedict's son, who was about nineteen, rowed over in the dinghy and started to explore the building. It had been a store, and under one roof were living quarters, a space open on each side for customers from boats and the store rooms. It almost looked as if the people had left without warning and propelled by sudden disaster. The floor of the kitchen was covered with old accounts books, complete with names and dates and scribbled orders. Many of them were dated in the year 1932, and Benedict, who had not lost his peasant's natural cynicism, wondered if the accounts had ever been paid.

We stood in a little group and tried to imagine how it would look if it was cleaned up and made habitable again. They would need plywood to line the walls, a stove, beds and chairs and a table. Benedict said that he could make most of the furniture himself, or, perhaps, borrow some things from friends on the nearby reserve. He and the boy went out to bring over the fishing boat while the two girls climbed the stairs to examine the bedrooms. In some strange and effortless way, while the sun beat down on the translucent sea, the old float house became home. When you or I might have swept and scrubbed and made impossible plans, Benedict simply steered the troller alongside and tied up. The girls sat on the outer logs with their legs dangling and their toes in the water. The things Benedict asked for were not what I would have chosen, but I did not argue. And we had to think of a way to get ten sheets of plywood from the town on the east coast of Vancouver Island, through the mountains to Gold River and down the fifty mile inlet and then across the final stretch of sea from where the weekly steamer called in. Luckily, the weather was good, and there was no sign of change.

I was reluctant to leave. It was not far by Cessna, flying at seven thousand feet and at one hundred and twenty miles an hour, from Nootka to my home, but the time and distance factors were unimportant. Nootka was a world of desultory awakening. Each moment there was like a drop of crystal clear water. Benedict was not worried; he knew that he could go down to the reserve and stay with friends. If, at a later date, people tried to get money out of the government for the provision of food and shelter, it was not Benedict to whom they sent demands. Hospitality was free, but the government was always available for milking. The government was a large cow with an expanding udder. Had it not been so constructed, there would have been no milk and no milking.

Meanwhile, I decided to go down to the reserve. I was in the right mood for conversations which started nowhere and ended nowhere and for arguments which I always lost.

That particular coast was often shrouded in white fog during the summer months. The fog burned off by noon, and it usually lay along the shoreline and up the inlets, rising to a height of five hundred feet. From the fog, the Pacific rolled in and broke on the rocks. Even on days when the surface was like glass, the ocean breathed in its depth, so that white surf poured across the outer reef. From a flying point of view, the fog was a nuisance. After crossing the mountains, we had to find a hole through which we could reach the sea. At times, we landed in a strip of sunlight and then taxied through the fog to our destination. Friendly Cove was less bothered by fog than some places farther to the north and west.

The sun was bright on the day I flew from Benedict's burned house to the reserve. Right under the floats was the Cook Channel, and other names were a reflection of history and imagination. Discovery Point was to the east; Santa Gertrudis Cove, the San Miguel Islands and Saavedra Island were to the west. I could see the village church ahead, and the rest of the buildings were scattered along the shoreline.

When you land there you walk on the boards of the new dock and pass a sign which reads: Welcome to Friendly Cove. The first house is on your left; it is very old and consists of two large rooms. The boards with which the house is built are a pale grey. Wind comes in at floor level. The old woman who lives there does not look forward to the winter. I spent many cheerful hours listening to her stories and watching her weaving the beautiful baskets of the coast culture.

Behind the house there was a flat stretch of green grass and then the blue of the Pacific. The spit on which the village had been built was narrow. With water on two sides and the rising slopes of the Nootka cedar forest to the north, the place was so different from the company towns that I became infatuated. Yet there was the usual sadness in the village. One hoped that the older Indians would live out their lives in peace and not be overwhelmed by a cataclysm of change and progress and disaster. The smaller children used their own language; they were dark eyed little extroverts who spent most of the summer days on the beach and enjoyed posing for photographs. I could never forget them, because their eventual fate was as certain as sunset. They would be flown away to the Catholic Residential School when they were six years old. Sometimes they would return for Christmas, but many would not see their parents again for a year. Some might advance to High School and would spend some unhappy and destructive years in a foster or boarding home in one of the small towns on the east coast of Vancouver Island.

I used to sit on the grass bank above the beach and watch the children, knowing that it was impossible to help them. Their destiny was already settled by the society into which they would move. In their own community, they were bright, eager children without fear or frustration. And I, too, could be with them for half a day and feel the tension drain away and the stress of the world be reduced to the small worry about encroaching fog. This is not to say that the place was perfect or that the people there did not suffer. The winter was long and filled with rain and high winds. People drank; they fought; they sometimes made one another's lives miserable. But whatever they did, the causes and effects were natural and conclusive. There were no hypocrites in the village. If a man disliked me or disliked what I represented or what I said or what I did, he would indicate his dislike. I tried to do the same.

Wilfred lived in a yellow house above the beach; he was not, in fact, the chief, but he had the short-wave radio in his house and was a responsible and articulate man for whom I had great respect. At first sight he looked battered by fate, because he used a crutch and had the face of a retired boxer. All Indians had experienced hardship, and Wilfred had suffered an attack of polio as a youth. He owned a boat in which he voyaged up the inlet when necessary. His courage was a natural attribute. His seamanship had been learned from experience.

As with most coast radios, the one at Friendly Cove was turned on for certain hours each evening, but it was possible to call out at any time. Reception was poor, and there were weeks when the generator broke down or the plant ran out of fuel. At such times, sick children were taken by boat to the hospital at Esperanza, but that was a long trip on a dark winter night with a high wind screaming down the mountain passes.

Not many months ago, Wilfred, with his wife and small son aboard, had left Gold River for Friendly Cove. It was a day of grey skies and cool winds. The first ten miles of the voyage was in the narrower part of the inlet, and the mountains rose straight out of the sea. There were few beaches, few breaks in the rock façade. There was snow on the northern slopes. Far ahead, the water was divided by an island, and it was possible to take either of the channels in order to continue towards the west. Wilfred steered to the south, passing close to the submerged hull of a ten thousand ton freighter which had been wrecked there in a rain storm. As usual, the strength of the wind increased towards the open sea.

Fifteen miles down the inlet, you come to a stretch of water which lies between Nootka Island and the indented coastline. It is about twenty-five square miles and is almost filled by Bligh Island and thirty smaller islands. The result is that the whole area is a confusion of rocks and navigable passages, the main channel to the sea running in a south-westerly direction for six miles before it reaches open water. It was somewhere in this channel that Wilfred's engine stopped. The boat was caught in the wind and the tide and forced towards the shore. There was no time for attempts to restart the engine. The water was too deep for anchoring. On such occasions, a seaman can only make sure that his passengers have life jackets and that anything that might float is unlashed for use in the water. Everything happened very quickly. The boat struck a rock, turned on its side and was smashed again and again as it was driven on to the shore of Bligh Island.

On the day of the wreck, Wilfred was returning from Vancouver where the little boy had been in hospital. So it is probable that the boy was weak. Also, Wilfred's wife was expecting a child. Many things passed through his mind when, for one of those long instants of time, he was trapped in the half submerged boat. He struggled to the surface. By the time he reached shore the boat had sunk. His wife and son were on the beach. He discovered that he was still holding his crutch in his right hand.

Wilfred does not talk very much about the four days he spent on the island. The first two days were cold and wet. They had no food, no matches to make a fire. Little could be salvaged from the boat, but Wilfred swam out several times and dived among the rocks to see if he could find a knife or an axe on the bottom. During the second night, his wife's baby was born. The child died. By the morning of the third day, Wilfred decided that he would go for help.

The tides around Nootka are strong, and a prediction of them is difficult. At the time of the flood, the entire Pacific Ocean rises fourteen feet, so that the sea comes up the strait and through the small passages, along inlets and into the coves and bays. The action takes place in the centre of the strait some time before the inlets are affected. Thus, the tide can be flooding in the centre and either ebbing or slack in the peripheral areas along the shore. During the forenoon, Wilfred sat on the rocks and watched the logs which floated past, paused and then returned as the tide changed. Apart from the movement of water up and down the strait, there was a flow and an ebb from the centre to the sides. A log which left Bligh Island during the flood would usually hit the same shore again to the north. If it left shore during the ebb it would float out into the middle of the strait and then be gripped in the strong pull towards the open sea.

Wilfred reckoned that if he was to cross the four miles of water between Bligh Island and Nootka he would have to start during the last two hours of the ebb. He would take with him the largest log he could find. At first, he would drift to the south, but, before he was swept out to sea, the tide would turn and he would, if lucky, be able to paddle into the western waters of the strait. He would cross the tidal watershed, so to speak. The six-hour flood would take him along the Nootka coast and drop him on a beach somewhere near the derelict cannery.

That is exactly what happened. He left his wife and son and kicked himself away from the shallow water. The twenty-foot log was under his stomach. He was at the mercy of the tides.

I met Wilfred and his wife after they were re-united in the mission hospital at Esperanza. They were feeling better and were holding hands as if they still doubted the fact of survival. Perhaps the greatest loss was the boat, for the people of the coastal islands used the water as a road. Now, there were only two boats left at Friendly Cove. The isolation would increase for the men, women and children who chose to remain in the village.

There were many hazards for the people of Friendly Cove. A team of archaeologists from a university had arrived to dig trenches in the village. I do not know whether anything interesting was found, but for several weeks there were fourteen-foot holes all over the place which were a danger at night. Sometimes the mail was held up by storms, and expected cheques did not arrive. There were occasions when Wilfred went out in his dinghy to catch a fish so that his family would eat. Teachers flew away at Christmas time and were unable to return for several weeks. The election of a new band council was held fifty miles away and half the village was disenfranchised by a fog. There was a small but unpleasant race war when two fishing boats tied up near Benedict's float house. The white crews became drunk during the night and decided that they liked the look of Benedict's three daughters who were, in fact, very attractive. Benedict loaded his rifle and sent his son for help. The fishermen pelted the float house with rocks and empty bottles and sailed away at dawn before the police arrived. And after all this, there were the less tangible hazards of reserve life.

The administration of land, housing, schools, medical care and council elections came under a Federal group of civil servants. Sometimes a man sitting in an office a hundred miles away would forget that the Indian men and women were Canadian citizens. They were not Displaced Persons, immigrants, children, prisoners, mental patients, mule deer or rainbow trout. They possessed certain rights over which the civil servants had no control. One of the young women of Nootka lost her husband in an industrial accident. A cheque for life insurance was sent to the Department of Indian Affairs, and a local official decided that the woman was not capable of handling her own affairs. Instead of forwarding the cheque to her, he placed it in a trust account and paid her a small sum every month from the account. He was surprised and angry when the young woman protested, and it took ten months to have his decision reversed. He never did understand what the argument was about.

In one way, I was also a hazard. My responsibilities included the administration of the Protection of Children Act, the Juvenile Delinquents Act and probation services in the area. One walked a thin and often unstable tightrope between the realities of Indian life and the requirements of the law. Some Indian children were physically neglected, but the wilful neglect of entire native villages for half a century by the white administration was no less serious.

The emotional neglect of an Indian child could only be appreciated if one knew the cultural background. There was always a danger that I would make a mistake and remove a child because I was ignorant or tired or bad tempered or impatient or persuaded.

Therefore, wandering between the houses in the village, I tried to forget the puritan world from which I came. The flight over the mountains sometimes helped because the cabin of the Cessna, suspended at fifteen thousand feet over snow slopes and passing between silent masses of cumulus, became a pressure chamber. I could enter in one frame of mind and acquire a new philosophy from the sky. It was more difficult on the return journey.

There was always an hour when some of us would sit in the afternoon sunshine to discuss the children who might need help in their education. A father, a mother, an aunt, a grandfather and myself would talk around the subject in an abstract sort of way. The father might ask questions about various schools. If I wanted to be positive, I said little. Meanwhile, a girl of eighteen sat on the edge of the group and looked at a magazine; she had her legs stretched out in front of her and her head was bent and she did not take part in the conversation. But she knew why I was there.

I said that more of the children were going to the public school instead of the Catholic schools.

"That's true," the girl's mother said. "I went to residential school myself."

"Did you like it?"

"It was all right."

"Nowadays the older girls and boys can go back to complete their education or to train as typists or nurses or to do hairdressing or anything else. Some choose art. Some music. There are good programmes."

"Is this for Indians?"

"For all young people who left school early."

"Residential school is too far away," the mother said.

"We could never afford to pay our children's fare home at Christmas."

"Do you have Christmas at home?"

"Yes. We have it like you white people."

"Our plan includes flying the students home for Christmas. Weather permitting, of course."

"The weather's bad in winter," the father said.

I was looking at the girl. She turned a page of her magazine. For many weeks, her mother had asked if I could find something for the girl to do. She simply sat around and listened to the radio or walked on the beach or lay in the sun. She had always done well at school. She had been top of her class and, at one time, had hoped to go to university. But something had gone wrong. No one knew why she had suddenly turned up on the reserve, how long she would stay or what she was thinking about. No one asked her questions about the future.

"Maria," I said. "What do you think of these plans?"

She raised her head and stared at me. "I don't know."

"Would you like me to keep a place for you in the up-grading course?"

This was a very direct question. Everyone looked away. I handed around my packet of cigarettes. Had I been with a white family I might have felt ashamed or stupid because the approach was so obvious. Be a good girl and go to school. Enter the social worker's Paradise. And had the girl not been Maria she might have agreed to take a course in order to get rid of me. People could manipulate one another out of their lives.

Maria turned a page in her magazine. She remained silent, but she was saying to me: "I have made my decision and will let you know about it when I feel like it."

I remained silent, but she knew that I answered: "We have all the time in the world."

We all sat there and looked at the water of the cove. Arctic terns were flying overhead and their narrow wings almost became invisible when they climbed across the white clouds to the blue sky. I felt very tense but pretended to forget my question which remained unanswered for so long. Five minutes. Ten minutes. Maria's father started to roll a cigarette. The grandfather sat very still, his lips compressed. A fly landed on his forehead but he did not move. Presently, Maria came to the last page of the magazine, leaned back and laughed at me, throwing the magazine to the ground. She laughed up at the sky. "O.K. Sure I'll take a course. When does it start?"

During the short winter days the ocean beyond Nootka was almost black with jade green surf on the wave tops. Much of the land along the coast was swamp, and from a plane you seemed to fly over endless patches of reflected sky. It rained often. We would come down out of the clouds and rock across the tree tops before touching down on the lake. It was not easy to land at the cannery, because the wings of the plane had to pass between posts and then avoid hitting the float house.

All the bits and pieces I had optimistically sent to Benedict had arrived, and he had lined one room with plywood and used a gas stove for cooking. The gales whistled overhead. The fishing boat was beached for annual repairs. When the winds were very strong the pilot would lower the flaps and close the throttle so that we hovered overhead like a great, blue eagle. It was not much of a performance but at least Benedict knew we tried. He did not really expect us to land. During his first winter there, the snow was heavy. Normally, the coast was warmed by the Japanese current, but that year the lakes were frozen and even the salt water inlets were covered with ice for many miles. The snow on the roof of the float house became soft and then froze again until it was an eight-inch layer of ice. For a while, Benedict thought that the weight of the snow would sink his home and he prepared to evacuate. He and his son had to chip away at the ice with an axe.

The children of Friendly Cove were no longer running

along the beach; they sat in the dark little houses, and if I visited them their eyes would reflect the grey daylight, and the world seemed depressing and frustrating. Sometimes a figure would be seated on a bed at the far end of the room, indistinct, silent. And rain beat against the windows or snow was driven down from the north. There was nothing to do. It might have been very different if there had been electricity there or if the people could have had a hot bath or if it had been possible to drive to a town. The teacher, whose name was Rafferty, continued to give lessons in the single classroom. The priest might come in for a funeral. I might arrive for a few hours to sit and talk and laugh with Josephine or Catherine or William or Robert.

There was always an empty house, and a month later I would run into the people who had left. They might be in the little mining town of Zeballos; they might be in Gold River; they might be in Vancouver or Victoria. And some would die, and there would be new graves beside the path to the beach. The young people continued to be married there. The church by the edge of the sea was well maintained; it had two beautiful stained glass windows which had been presented by the government of Spain. Friendly Cove was no longer of importance to seamen; it was forgotten as a place of historical interest; it was not even a centre of Indian life. However, for me, the village was a place where people lived. I had no desire to be some kind of Freudian bureaucrat, more interested in the past than the present and only concerned with the hidden roots of human problems. The frustrations were numerous and acute. They were there at the precise moment I stepped out of the plane into the driving rain. There were frustrations over lack of opportunity, over disinterest in what work there was, over friendships, marriages and children. The people could not derive much satisfaction from being Indians in a white world, nor could they become white. In any case, my only concern was to alleviate the immediate distress in the heart or the mind of one individual. If one person discovered greater satisfaction in life, even for a short time, my flight across the mountains was worthwhile.

Benedict's two school-age daughters had been home for Easter. I flew over to bring them back to the boarding home from which they went to school. We had crossed the mountains in a clear sky and were still at six thousand feet as we passed over the eastern coast of Nootka Island. Looking down, I could see the float house, but there was no sign of the white fishing boat. A few minutes later, we landed and taxied into the shade of the cedars. Benedict was at home; he told me that his boat was beached nearby. It was a bright, blue day with a light wind off the sea, and the tops of the cedar trees moved back and forth against the sky. The float house had become a real home; it had survived a winter and had protected the family through the worst of the snow and gales. Some nights had been uncomfortable, even dangerous. The whole place had listed fifteen degrees after one blizzard. It also moved against the rocks when the east winds blew down Muchalet Inlet.

We sat in the main room. Benedict's son had returned from a futile job in a logging camp and was painting a picture on a square of plywood. Benedict had carved three fine masks; he showed me a head mask which had belonged to his grandfather and was supposed to portray the captain of the first European vessel to arrive off Estevan Point. The two girls were packing; they had a lot of presents for the people with whom they lived. Benedict mentioned that the winter had been hard, but there had been many deer along the shore at dawn and he had been able to shoot some from the float. This year they planned to can salmon. There was ample fresh water in the old cannery pipe. Fuel for the stove could be bought in Zeballos. Life was pleasant. There was nothing he needed as long as the girls were educated.

Benedict and his wife left to work on the boat, and I watched them cross the island while the two girls climbed into the plane. The oldest daughter stood on the float to wave goodbye. She was at home for a visit and normally worked in Vancouver. I tried to imagine her in the city but failed. Alone on that ancient log raft, she looked very beautiful, a black-haired Cinderella who retained the grace and charm of her race. Many months later, I learned that her prince had arrived, for she had married an Englishman and was living in Manchester.

Those things that were good about life on a reserve were probably lost if a family moved to the city. Things that were bad were lost, too. Perhaps the worst of it was that the people thought they were lucky to live on public assistance in a derelict house in a city slum. The price of integration was terrible. Neighbours complained to the police and to the Child Welfare Agencies. Sometimes the children had to be kept indoors throughout the long summer days. The good white people on the street complained that the value of their property went down if there were Indians next door. Had I been a man of Nootka I would have taken my family back to the coast, to the isolation, the winds and the rain and the old, frame houses and the one-room school. If I lacked courage and patience to face endless humiliation the Indian did not. Such was the requirement of his survival.

## 15

# The World of Julia Charlie

HOME is a four-roomed house in a small village forty miles from the nearest town, telephone and doctor. Home is an environment. You walk along between the houses and Julia stands waiting. She is tall and quiet, not exactly herself at this meeting any more than you are yourself. The identity distortion is like the refraction of the sun's rays; it is unimportant if appreciated.

"Good morning, beautiful Julia. So you wish to be a nurse. And have you ever had TB?"

"Oh, no."

"Have you ever been in hospital?"

"Let me see. Yes I have."

"Long ago?"

"Yes."

"What year?"

"Last year."

"Was it anything serious?"

She starts laughing. "Just a little TB."

A conversation with Julia. It is very funny. And how is it that the little child who was born in the village where houses are small and overcrowded and parents are supposed to drink and fight has grown into such a charming and sophisticated young woman? She may be fourteen or sixteen or eighteen. She is mature. Legally a child. What exactly does she want out of life? Who is she and what is she? To answer this it is necessary to find out what has happened to her.

Today she is shy and modest, gay, quiet, determined, incurious and self-sufficient; she is a character of contradictions. Her life is a series of small moments in the present tense, not only in fact but also in her mind and even in her dreams. She is watchful and distrustful, disliking questions and indifferent to the future. She has many loyalties.

She was born in a small, green cabin. The one west of the church. She is the oldest in the family, having four brothers and two sisters. Two other children died in infancy. Julia's father was drowned five years ago as were an uncle and a second cousin. Death is a constant ceremony in Julia's life, and she has no fear.

Julia spent her first three winters and her first four summers with a grandmother. The home was secure and warm. She was handled a great deal and fed when she was hungry. Her first memory is of being thrown into the water as a small child. She learned to swim early in life. Her first words were Indian. All her early thoughts were Indian thoughts.

Julia was four when her grandmother died; she went to live with her parents in the overcrowded cabin next to the church. Her father was often ill. At such times the family income was eighty-seven dollars a month, assistance being provided at the rate of fifteen dollars a month for the mother and twelve dollars each for the children. The family received a clothing allowance twice a year.

Julia and her two sisters slept in the same bed. They had a mattress but only one blanket. They slept in their clothes. There was no water piped to the cabin. The children carried buckets from a stand pipe two hundred feet down the village road. It was the familiar face of rural poverty but for Julia's parents there was no thought of poverty which is only known by comparison. Julia's inheritance was harsh, but there was no self-pity in her family. There was unity and coherence made necessary by the struggle to survive. They did not know of poverty but they understood need; they were not possessive. The family shared in the struggle and, if successful, turned to help others who were less fortunate. In the end, of course, the man who could give the greatest help to his friends and neighbours was obviously the best man in the community.

A man looking from a car might glance down towards Julia's home and see the environment of deprivation. The white man would pity the children and accuse the parents. He would conclude that such conditions resulted from unemployment or inability to use money correctly. But Julia would simply see the car go past on the highway and it would only be a moving car. Nothing else.

She learned by her fifth birthday that every member of the family had certain duties and obligations. She also learned not to interfere with her brothers and sisters. Once she could walk and talk she was expected to help in the house and to manage her own thoughts and actions outside the family circle. She was never punished and she rarely showed emotion. A crying child could spoil the hunt today as in the old days it could upset an ambush. The family was a group who shared the same roof and usually slept in the same room but learned to avoid one another's private affairs.

The small village of wooden houses was created for good and practical reasons. In past years, the nomadic tribe followed game and moved to a fishing camp on the river bank in the summer. Missionaries travelled in summer time. Thereafter the first churches were built near the fishing camps. It followed naturally that the first land granted to the Indians was an acreage near and including the camp. For a generation the village on the reserve was a more or less permanent camp, and houses were not considered to be of much value. The people liked to be warm and dry, but it was some time before they felt the need of furniture and other possessions. A large house was difficult to heat and partitions inside the house simply cut off heat from the stove.

Julia's inheritance and her environment mingled to form the foundation of a new culture. The normal and sensible behaviour of her parents had created the environment in which she lived. But within thirty years this environment was creating behaviour patterns which were socially unsound.

In the eyes of the white man the Indian village became identified with a slum, a place of poverty and alcoholism. It was also thought to be a bad thing for the Indians to live in separate communities. Would it not be better if they left their reserves and were educated for some of the jobs available in urban settings?

The Indian had other ideas. He did not oppose the white man's viewpoint because he neither understood nor considered it. He liked the village of his ancestors and did not feel confined, for he had trap lines in the surrounding hills, hunted over hundreds of square miles, had only to wait for the fish to swim up from the sea and, in any case, felt more secure at home. He did not see himself as an object of pity or concern. He came from a distinctive and original society and he knew that what strengths remained in his community were of his own culture.

Julia's early view of life was one sided. Her parents had been given a little education in a school on the reserve. Both the school teacher and the priest were white, but the child's life was controlled by native custom and thought. Thus, her first term at school was not only an introduction to education; it brought to her the philosophy of the white civilisation.

To a girl who was taught to be free and independent within the family circle, the teacher was surprising and extraordinary. He asked many questions; he was curious and he often appeared to be rude. If any of the children were late, the teacher would send a letter to the parents as if they were responsible. The teacher also complained if the children were dirty or if they lost their books.

This particular teacher stayed in the village for a year. And during the next six years of Julia's education there were seven different teachers. The last of these was a young woman who became fond of Julia and asked the girl to live in the apartment attached to the school.

"I don't know," Julia said.

"Would you like to come and live with me?"

"Yes," the girl said.

At this time, her father was away in hospital. Her mother was often unhappy and when she was unhappy she drank. The unhappiness was caused by uncertainty and confusion. In the old days it was possible to live well by trapping, fishing, digging clams, hunting and cutting poles. Now there was a change. It was necessary to have money to survive, and, as each year passed, more money was needed. Children going to school asked for clothes. The way of life was changing and the old language, having no economic base, was not used so often. The old culture was important in the village, but it was only important to those who understood it.

The teacher walked down to see Julia's mother.

The older houses were of log construction and the floors some six feet above the ground. Julia's family had a new, four-roomed frame house supplied by the government. It was a fragile building. In the front room the furniture consisted of an old chesterfield, a wood stove for cooking, a round, metal heating stove and a table. There were three beds in the house. That was all. Lighting came from oil lamps suspended from the ceiling. One window was broken. There was nowhere to store food, nowhere for the children to do their homework. There were no books. The only gesture to leisure hours was a small transistor radio.

The teacher was horrified and said: "I was wondering if you would let Julia come to live with me for a while. You must be crowded here."

"I don't know. You had better ask her."

Julia's mother was quite proud of the new house. Until recently the family had lived in one room.

The teacher said. "Julia would like to come to me."

"If she wants to . . ." the woman said.

It was not a satisfactory conversation, but that evening Julia took her belongings up to the school. She had a room of her own and found it very pleasant to sit by herself and look out of the window. But she felt strange. There was no laughter, none of the usual freedom.

The teacher was worried by the girl's aloofness and wrote in her diary: "The poor child is probably emotionally disturbed. She is withdrawn, and it may take me some time to become her friend."

It was three weeks before Julia started to sit with the teacher in the evenings and by that time the situation had changed. One morning Julia heard that her mother was not well and needed help at home. Julia said nothing to the teacher; she packed and went home. She did not attend school for a week. From time to time, she was seen carrying water and hanging clothing on the line. She seemed happy.

It was a hot summer. Julia did not object to helping at home. In the evenings she ran along the shore to a remote cove where the children swam and sat and talked by the water's edge. She had forgotten all about the teacher, all about school. In any case, holidays were to start in a week, and the teacher would be leaving. In the fall, there would be another stranger in the school.

Julia's father died in July. The body was brought back from the hospital, and the village was filled with friends and relatives who came for the funeral. The dead man had been related to a well-remembered chief who had been influential in keeping the community together in the past. In fact many people would have been surprised to know that the small, sick and illiterate man had been powerful. People had feared him. He had been listened to in the community although no one from outside took any notice of him whatsoever. Outsiders usually talked to those Indians who went to church or were thought to be intelligent in terms of school records or who had material possessions. Few of these people had much influence in the community.

It was left to Julia and her generation to have daily and continual contact with both white and Indian ideas. The girl was twelve and a half years old; she was still quiet and shy, but she had learned from the teacher that there was an alternative way of life. It seemed to be a strange and sometimes pointless life, but it was an alternative.

On her thirteenth birthday Julia is a tall, slim girl with a fringe and hair to her shoulders. She is outgrowing the local school, and her attendance is poor. She still sleeps in her clothes and is now looking after her mother for much of the time. She is more independent than ever. Her diet is poor. She is obedient when asked to remain at home, because she is required by the family. She does not complain. Once a month she drinks a few glasses of beer. She reads magazines and likes teenage music from America.

The new teacher is European, used to poverty and used to political moves to get rid of poverty. He is neither a socialist nor a humanist but he has lived so long in the European scene that he does not accept deprivation and need. He knows that Julia exists and that she should be at school. He meets her mother. In such a small village it is surprising that he does not meet Julia for four months. Meanwhile he has reported her poor school attendance to the authorities and her family allowance has been stopped. Julia's mother is very angry.

"Why has the family allowance been stopped?"

"Because Julia is not at school," the teacher says.

"She cannot go to school without clothes and books."

"You send her along."

"I am sick. I need her at home."

"Perhaps some older girl . . ."

"How could I pay an older girl?"

"You get help from the government?"

"Eighty-seven dollars a month. For seven of us. Could you live on that?"

"All right," the teacher says. "I'll see what I can do."

"Julia goes out at night too much."

The teacher says: "Have you spoken to her about it?"

"No. Could you speak to her?"

"I might."

"You speak to her. She should be in at night."

"Does she get into trouble?"

"I don't know."

The teacher sends for Julia, who turns up after two days. She is guarded and indifferent. She has delayed visiting the school as long as possible and has confided in her friends that the teacher is an old goat. She is inwardly amused, but her appearance is sullen. It takes her a little time to understand what the teacher means.

"Ah, Julia. I'm glad you were able to come. Is your mother well?"

No answer.

"What about these late nights, eh?"

Julia's mind adjusts to the new situation. Many of the older girls are beginning to disagree with some of the native customs whereby a girl does much of the work in the home while the mother relaxes and has babies. Nowadays the family can survive without such a custom.

The teacher does not understand what is involved. He does not appreciate that he is being used to bolster the discipline of the family and he imagines that it is Julia's personal and private life which is being questioned.

"You should be in at night, Julia. This village . . ."

She looks at the floor. She is trying to think of something else, of catching salmon or swimming.

"I could really use you in school, Julia."

No answer.

"You were doing very well. Didn't you like school?"

"Yes." It is the polite answer.

"You will come back then?"

"Yes."

"And stay in at night to do your homework?"

"Yes."

"Good. I'm sure we will get on very well."

Outside, Julia walks slowly away until she turns a corner and is hidden from view. Then she runs like an antelope towards the beach and catches up with her friends who are walking on the shore. They ask no questions. She laughs with them at a hidden joke. Within a few minutes she has forgotten all about the teacher.

It is a Sunday afternoon. In Julia's home a man is drinking; he is already drunk. He has been fighting. A man without a woman in an Indian community is almost useless particularly if he has a job nearby or has children. So a man has come to live with Julia's mother. He takes little interest in the children. Julia says nothing, but she moves to the home of an aunt. She simply packs her brown paper parcels and walks to the aunt's home and sits down. No one asks any questions. The aunt may not want Julia there but she does not say so. This is the way tension within a family is relieved, and it works very well.

Meanwhile the visiting priest and the teacher have been

discussing Julia and her family. It is decided to report the situation to the Department of Social Welfare.

Drinking in the home continues until the man leaves for work on Tuesday morning, a day late. By this time he has experienced two days of heroism, superiority and, to a certain extent, infallibility. He has been a man with an identity. All this evaporates at dawn on Tuesday.

The social worker comes to the village once a month, mainly to see old people about their pensions. He flies in aboard a silver and scarlet float plane. He is young, about twenty-five. He has a large caseload and relies for information about people on the Superintendent of the Indian Agency.

He has with him a letter about Julia written by the teacher. The letter complains that Julia is not going to school and is living a wild life and being taken advantage of by young men and boys. The mother is often drunk. The man now living in the home is usually unemployed. Is the girl in need of protection?

Julia's own position and her own thoughts about the situation are becoming clarified. Apart from the weakening of Indian culture, there had arisen in many families the natural tensions between the old generation and the new. Julia's ideas were a combination of many things and derived from many influences. She was unique in that the Indian girls of her generation were the first to live in two worlds; they did not simply move from Indian to white or from the old to the new, but divided their lives between two very strong and positive cultures.

The social worker is short of time; he has chartered a plane for four hours and has eight stops to make and fifteen people to visit.

He walks up through the wind and the rain and the mud. Past the graveyard. He sees the graves of small children who have died of sickness and graves of the old people who have died naturally. And there are the graves of the middle aged. Death by accident.

It is warm in Julia's home and the social worker watches his coat steam. The woman says:

"Julia? She's at her aunt's."

"Well . . . Can't you make her go to school?"

"You could speak to her."

"Yes."

"We don't get the family allowance."

"No. Not while Julia stays away from school."

"But how can I send her without clothes?"

The social worker looks at the small children and walks in the rain to the house of the aunt. The aunt says:

"We don't want her here, really. We have no room."

"Have you spoken to her mother?"

"No."

"What does Julia say?"

"I don't know. Could you ask her how long she will be here?"

"Didn't she tell you?"

"No."

"It's about school . . ."

"I don't know," the aunt says. "She has left school, I think."

"Well . . . Where is Julia now?"

"She went over to the store."

The store is five miles away across the water, and boats from the village collect supplies except when the weather is exceptionally stormy. The social worker thanks the aunt and walks back to the home of the mother. The woman greets him as if she has not seen him for weeks.

"Yes," she says. "Julia went over to the store on my husband's boat. You know. The man who lives here now."

"Did he take her?"

"Oh, she went on the boat. I can't do anything with that girl. I need her to help me with the small kids."

"Do you think that Julia might do better in a foster home?"

"You should send her away. She does not do what I ask her."

"Did you tell her to go to school?"

"It's up to her."

The social worker says: "All right. I'll go and talk to her."

The woman smiles.

It is a short flight to the store. There is nothing much to see, a government dock and a lighting plant and a few fishing boats tied up alongside, the store and four or five cabins that are rented to sportsmen in the summer. The store is a large wooden building filled with a sepulchral gloom. Several people are looking at the counters. The store owner says:

"Julia? She came over this morning. Had a beer or two. She wants me to give her a job."

"Where is she now?"

"Down on the boat."

The boat is a twenty-eight-foot gill-netter, in need of a coat of paint. Below the wheelhouse there is a small cabin. The girl sits up and stares towards the light. A young man is fast asleep on one of the bunks.

She comes up on deck, tucking her shirt into her blue jeans. She looks towards the shore.

"Hello, Julia."

"Hello."

"Did you know that the teacher is very disappointed in you?"

"I want a job."

"You're still a child."

She remains impassive, withdrawn.

The social worker says: "You're not staying at home now?"

"That man. He drinks too much. I won't stay there. He bothers me."

"So you moved to your aunt's?"

"I want to go to town."

"You'd better go home first."

"I won't go back to the village."

The social worker asks:

"Who's that man down there?"

"What man?"

"In the boat."

"That's George. He's my cousin."

"Do you like him?"

"He's all right."

There is a silence. The social worker is thinking. He does not know what to do with a young woman who is legally a child and is a free individual in many ways and a rebellious slave in others. She observes him with interest. He says:

"George looks after you."

"Yes."

"Well . . ."

"He's better than most of the boys. They wait for me at night in the village."

"Can't you stay in at night?"

Julia shrugs. "There's nothing to do."

"All right," the social worker says. "Get your things. I'll take you back to town with me."

She is not surprised and moves away with matter-of-fact elegance.

The foster parents are white, middle class, Protestant. They are apprehensive but eager to help. This is the first time they have had in their home an Indian child. They hear the car arrive and see the social worker come up to the door followed by a little girl with black hair. She wears a blue jacket and white jeans. The foster parents open the door and introductions are made.

Julia follows them into the living room and sits down. She does not look around her and seems incurious and detached. She is shown her bedroom, the kitchen, bathroom and basement. A fifteen-foot boat is parked on a trailer by the back door. The house is typical, furnished sparsely from a catalogue, very clean and bright. A small, white child stares at Julia from one corner.

The foster parents fuss around while the social worker makes out clothing and medical forms. The foster mother says:

"I'm sure you'll be very happy here. We are only a block from school and there are a lot of children to play with."

Julia looks out of the window. When the social worker leaves she follows him with her eyes. Later she sits opposite the foster mother during a meal; she eats very little; she goes into her room and sits on the bed. A boy of ten comes in and asks her if she wants to play. She shakes her head. The foster mother comes in and talks. Then the foster father. Then a small child. Julia sits in silence. Why can't they leave her alone?

For five weeks Julia has a new identity and is stimulated by the change. She goes to the public school where she is plainly out of her depth in the grade to which she is assigned. She remains polite and silent in the foster home but answers questions about life in the village. From time to time she meets old friends in town. She feels warmed by contact with them, by laughter and recognised faces.

On the whole, she dislikes the white girls of her own age, finding them cold and preoccupied with themselves. They are possessive and competitive; they have very different rules where personal relationships are concerned.

The concentration on the future and on outward appearance and on arbitrary values is alien to Julia. She thinks more and more of her own home, her own world. She misses the gaiety and humour; she even misses the release of inhibitions through alcohol. She has come from a warm, violent and demanding world to one where emotions are controlled and where she is treated as a child. Her world is one of endurance; it is concerned with survival. She understands the intense and rigid disciplines of a patriarchal society, a discipline mixed with lack of interference. Thus she might seek love from a young man if she is old enough but will not be permitted to marry if she is still needed at home. Yet she is still an individual and if she rebels and leaves home she will no longer be a part of the family. After that, her visits to her home will be few and she will be an uninvited guest.

She is very much alone. Between puberty and marriage she will join with other girls of her own age who are existing in the half light, neither child nor woman. As a result of her upbringing, she will seek affection. She has, so to speak, been trained for marriage.

The foster home is a façade; it does not provide complete security and, after two months, it fails to stimulate. Once again, her identity becomes uncertain. It will take five years at least in the white world before she stops thinking as an Indian girl.

In the month before the fishing season many of the village boats are tied up at the town dock. Julia's uncle is there. George is there. Three of her girl friends walk along the streets in the evening, and Julia meets them. She goes back to the boat with them and they all sit on one of the bunks and talk. George has a few bottles of beer which are drunk without having much effect. It is a social evening at first. It is a night of relaxation and release and forgetfulness.

Julia walks back to the foster home in the early hours of the morning. It is obvious she has been drinking. She is neither defensive nor repentant.

A week later the social worker visits Julia's mother who says: "I hear Julia is drinking in town. I thought you were supposed to be looking after her."

She sits on her bed in the foster home and decides to run away. On the other side of the closed bedroom door the family watch television. She has withdrawn from them all. No one understands her. Neither the foster mother, nor the school counsellor, nor the social worker are providing her immediate needs; they can only talk about tomorrow, about the future. But she needs a life in the present tense and she needs affection which is simple and direct and intensely personal.

In the morning she leaves for school but walks down to the dock. Her uncle's boat is ready to leave. She climbs aboard. No one pays much attention to her. It is a grey day and there is a strong wind, but she is not afraid. If the boat sinks they will all try to swim to the shore. She sits in the cabin, the uninvited guest. And after a while someone asks her if she is hungry.

"We did everything we could," the foster mother tells the social worker. "We treated her as if she was our own child. But she would never talk to us and spent half the time in her room. She must be seriously disturbed, poor girl. When you think of the conditions of her home life . . . terrible. Some of those people should be brought into court. They should not be permitted to have children."

From where George and Julia sit on a grassy slope on the edge of the timber line, the whole village can be seen at a glance. The inlet of blue water comes from the distance, and, close at hand, is the sickle beach. A sandy road winds over the hillside, leading, it seems, from nowhere to nowhere. The houses spread out around the top of the beach. It looks a tight little community of people who think and behave alike.

Julia, observing it, knows differently; she knows that the village is a number of families, friends and enemies, those who are loved and those who are hated. It is a community of dissension. Under the red roof, for instance, is a family who have a big boat, three sons of working age and two daughters to help at home. They are comparatively rich; they have learned how to make money and they make it by selling things and services to others less fortunate. Under the brown roof are the poorest people, a middle-aged couple with nine children. And so it is, roof after roof.

George is in love with Julia; he feels responsible and

possessive and very old. He smiles at her. Whatever else might happen, they have each other. Meanwhile, Julia will follow tradition. She will serve her mother until she serves a husband. In between she has the loneliness of complete freedom if she defies the village customs. The only other way is to escape from the village and try her luck in the white world.

That evening, without telling George or her mother, Julia writes a long letter to the social worker.

Social workers come and go. The new one is a young woman with a brand new B.A.; she is twenty-three. She reads Julia's letter and asks advice from the Indian Superintendent, who says that Julia should be at school. The social worker writes a brief note to Julia to remind the girl that she should be at school. Then the file is put away because unless there is a suspicion of neglect the affairs of young Indian girls are not the responsibility of the Department of Social Welfare.

However, the social worker visits Julia's mother in the village some time later. The mother is not well, Julia is washing the floor.

"I hear Julia wants a job," the social worker says.

"I need her here."

"She should finish her education."

"She wouldn't go back to school."

"It seems a pity."

"The teacher was no use, anyway."

The social worker asks Julia: "Do you still want a job?"

"No," Julia says.

"Well . . . Let me know when you do."

Julia watches the young woman leave. The floor is half washed. Her mother goes to lie down on the bed; she is expecting a baby. The other children run indoors and leave dirty footprints all over the floor.

In the evening it starts to rain. Julia walks away from the village and intercepts one of the trucks coming down the logging road from the upper camp. She rides twenty miles in the truck and is left at a camp on the water's edge and waits an hour and a half before she is offered a boat ride to the town. She hopes to find George, who is working in a sawmill on the north side of the town. She has no money and hopes to travel eighty miles in all. She wears a thin summer dress. By late evening it is cool, and she is in the half-deserted streets of the town. She knows nobody, but there are Indian families living out by the river, and she heads that way.

At dusk, she is given a ride by a young man who sees through her weariness and shabbiness to her beauty. He also imagines that she will be accommodating. He gives her a cup of coffee in a roadside store. She drinks the coffee slowly, because the moment is valuable and fleeting. Love and affection are like sunlight to her. She is ready. She knows little of the law, and, in any case, the law is meaningless when compared to her emotions and desires.

It is dark when they drive on towards the north, the town lights behind them. Rain falls, and a wind blows in from the sea.

Julia is silent, because she is half afraid. No longer is she a free individual protected within a tight, cultural barrier. She is in a larger world and is unable to see its boundaries.

"Have you got a name?" the young man asks.

"Yes."

"I bet it's Mary."

"No."

"Why not tell me?"

"Julia."

"Julia what?"

No answer.

"Oh, all right. Where are you going?"

"To my cousins."

"Out here in the bush?"

"Is this your car?" Julia asks.

"Yes."

"Where do you live?"

"You ask a lot of questions, don't you?"

She turns her head away and looks out of the window.

Five miles north of the town the young man stops the car and lights a cigarette. "Smoke?"

She shakes her head.

"What about a drink?"

The young man produces a bottle from under the front seat and unscrews the top. "Here. It's quite harmless."

Julia is used to being told what to do. She does not like the taste of the wine, but she drinks because she does not like an argument. She is obedient and matter-of-fact. She says:

"I don't like drinking."

"Makes you feel good. Have another."

She tips back the bottle and lets a little of the wine roll on to her tongue. The young man is affectionate. He puts an arm around her. She is passive, but she does not want to be put out into the rain.

They do not hear the police car or see the constable until he opens the door and uses his flashlight. The young man is cool and unafraid. Julia is withdrawn, for the intrusion and interference of strangers is alien. She does not understand.

"How old are you?" the constable asks.

She does not answer.

The young man says: "She told me she was eighteen."

"Oh? What's her name?"

"Julia."

"Julia what?"

"I don't know."

Julia is thinking of something else; she is very alert, but her mind does not permit thoughts of danger. She simply wishes that the constable will go away and that the present can continue.

"Could I see your licence, sir?" the constable asks.

Julia sits well back in the shadows and looks out at the falling rain. The world into which she has strayed seems to be an unreal world of fantasy and endless questions. It is a world of little partitions. It confronts her like a faceless wall, and she retreats, knowing that whatever else might happen to her there is another world to which she can return.

"Come on," the constable says to her. "We'll take you home."

She does not move. "I'm not going home."

"Well, you'd better come with us."

"It's all right," the young man says.

"I'm going to my cousins."

"Come along," the constable says quietly. "We'll take you home."

She follows him through the darkness without looking back at the young man. During the drive to town she is silent in the back of the police car and she is silent when she sits in the police office. After half an hour the young woman from the Department of Social Welfare arrives, smiling.

"Julia. What a night to be out."

Julia looks at the floor. She knows that this moment will pass and that something else will happen. She knows that if she waits long enough something better will take place. She has only to wait. Sooner or later they will all go away and leave her alone.

"We'll have to get you home, Julia," the social worker says cheerfully.

"I'm not going home."

"Did you know your mother was worried about you?"

No answer.

"Is there something wrong at home?"

No answer.

"Well . . . Come along. We'll see."

Julia hesitates. She does not trust people she cannot understand. She does not understand them because they are not members of her family and she does not see why they are interested in her. They are remote.

She feels that it would be better to leave the police office and stands up. The social worker opens the door.

"Come along, Julia."

It is very dark outside. Julia slips away. She hears the

social worker's quick shout, but after a while the only sounds are her own breathing and her footsteps and the rainfall on the road.

She runs to the south and decides that it is time to go home.

The truck passes the village in the morning and Julia jumps down. She walks across to her home, climbs the steps to the house and sits down with a bang in the corner of the old chesterfield. Her mother glances at her. The small children smile at her. Presently, because she is very tired, she goes across to the bedroom and lies down and pulls a blanket over herself. In five minutes she is fast asleep.

A week later the social worker arrives in the village and calls in to see Julia's mother.

"I'm glad Julia arrived home."

"She's here," the mother says.

"Isn't she happy here?"

"I don't know. She won't do anything I tell her."

"Why did she leave home?"

"You can ask her."

"She said nothing to you?"

"No."

The social worker shrugs. "It's a difficult age."

The mother says: "I can't do anything with her."

Julia listens to the conversation but she is concerned only with herself. A few words by a stranger only concern her indirectly. Talk about life is not life and talk about love is not love. Meanwhile she is again a part of the family.

After a while the social worker leaves. It grows dark outside. Julia goes off to the house of a friend, and the two girls sit and listen to music. On her way home a boy comes out suddenly from behind a building and pushes Julia to the ground. She struggles in silence, succeeds in escaping and runs to her house. An hour later, the man with whom Julia's mother is living moves silently through the house. He comes

to Julia's bed and puts his hand on her body. She is afraid
and lies rigid. She knows that her mother is awake, listening.
No one speaks. The moment is one of tension. Presently, the
man goes away. Julia climbs out of bed and leaves the house.
She sits shivering on the step outside, staring gloomily at the
viscid waters of the bay.

It is a week after Julia's sixteenth birthday, and it is
snowing. There is little sign of life in the village. Only the
dogs move, and smoke comes from the chimneys. The
constable passes the church and stops at the house. He
knocks and goes inside and stands near the door, snow
dripping from his boots on to the floor. The man is lying on
a bed; he does not move. Julia's mother says:

"He's sick. That's why he couldn't come to court."

"Sick?" the constable looks at the man. "The doctor
say so?"

"What doctor?"

"The doctor in town."

"I've no money to go to town."

"The case has been adjourned."

"I can't get into town," the man says.

"A man charged you with assault, you know."

"He hit me first."

"Yes. That's what the court will find out . . ."

"What are you going to do about my daughter?" the
woman says to change the subject.

"About Julia."

"She's going to have a baby."

"Where is she?" the constable glances around.

"At her aunt's."

"She's going to have a baby, eh?"

"Yes."

"You should do something," the man says.

"How old is she?"

"Sixteen last week."

"And who is the baby's father?"

No answer.

"Do you know?"

"You go and ask Peter."

"Peter? Isn't he married?"

"Yes."

"All right," the constable says. "I'll talk to him." He turns to go. "Where is Peter now?"

"Right in there," the man says.

"In the bedroom?"

"He's sleeping."

"He's living here, then?"

"No."

"Well, why doesn't he sleep in his own house?"

"I don't know."

"You let him stay here?"

The man says: "You better talk to him. We don't want him here. He's got his own house."

The people of an Indian Community are permissive; they do not interfere with one another. Yet they use outsiders when they become worried. Several people, including the social worker and the local magistrate, began to receive letters about Julia. Peter's wife wrote a letter. Julia's mother wrote a letter. Julia remained silent, self-sufficient and watchful. She was a fatalist.

Julia's mother is in hospital with a broken arm, and the common-law husband is charged with assault. He is given a suspended sentence and waits in town for three days. Then he and Julia's mother return home with a gallon of wine to celebrate their reunion. When they have finished the wine, the man again beats the woman, breaking her teeth. She returns to hospital and he is charged again and sentenced to four months in gaol. The woman attends the trial; she weeps silently when the man is led away.

The social worker visits the home and speaks to Julia:

"Well, Julia. You will be all right for a while. Your mother will be here with you and the other children."

"It wasn't fair."

"What wasn't fair?"

"My mother reported him."

"Well, after all, he beat her twice."

"She talks too much."

"Don't you think he should be in gaol?"

"They were drinking. That's why he did it."

"But you didn't like him, did you?"

"He's all right."

"What about yourself? What are you going to do?"

"Stay here."

"All right. Would you write to me if I can help in any way?"

"I'm all right." Julia speaks sullenly. She stands up and walks out of the room and down the road, her black hair shining in the pale winter sunlight.

The village looks small, but to those who live there it is a broad city. A girl will live in one house and, perhaps, visit relations. She will rarely step inside other homes. She might not speak to members of other families for months. Some of the people are successful; they own boats and sawmills. Of these, a few have crossed the cultural watershed and think like white men. Many think only Indian thoughts.

A girl comes home after eight years in the city; she has passed grade 12. She is glad to be back among her own people but says:

"I wouldn't like to stay here. There's nothing to do."

"Have you many friends here?"

"No. Very few."

"Do you know Julia?"

"Yes."

"But she isn't a friend of yours."

"I see her quite often."

"Is she happy?"

"Happy? I don't know if she is happy."

"Does she want to leave here?"

"Sometimes. But she gets homesick. I used to be homesick when I went away first."

"How long were you homesick?"

"Until I was eighteen."

"Julia has troubles at home."

"Yes. It's too bad. People don't understand each other, you know."

"What's going to happen to the baby?"

"It would be better adopted."

She is ashamed of being pregnant. She is also insecure. What will happen when she returns home? Her mother is too sick to care for a baby. Her uncle would keep the child if it turns out to be a boy. In fact many people in the village will be happy to have an extra baby in the home providing it receives support from the Department. But if she keeps the baby herself she will have to support it.

All the white people talk about adoption. Peter seems to be proud that he is the father, but he does not talk about the future. George does not talk to her very much now; he is a friend of Peter's. However, he is still a man with whom she can discuss her problems.

"Even if I did marry you," George says, "I don't want to support the baby. I wouldn't want it around here."

"My aunt will look after it," Julia says.

"We don't want it around here."

"No," she says. "All right."

They are sitting on the edge of the dock where the fishing boats lie under the spring sunshine. Julia looks away across the water. Across the green foothills and the blue mountains is the town. She does not know the town well, but she remembers the social worker and the foster parents. People over there think strangely but they all have different thoughts. In the village and in her home there is only one single thought. Her mother can only see life in one image, one pattern. The single thought is hard and very distinct and unchanging. There is no relief.

She looks sideways at George and says:

"I think I'll go away for a while."

"Please yourself."

"We could get married later."

"We could."

"I can get the baby adopted."

George says: "My father doesn't want me to get married."

"Why not?"

"I don't know."

"We could move away."

"Where to?"

"Somewhere. Anywhere."

He shrugs. "It isn't easy."

Julia stands up. "I'm going to write some letters."

"Carry on," George says.

There is a new social worker, a middle-aged woman who is bemused by a caseload of three hundred and fifty. Julia comes into the office and sits down; she does not speak. The social worker glances at the file.

"You are from the reserve?"

"Yes," Julia says.

"You don't come here for help, you know. Have you written to the Indian Superintendent?"

"No."

"Is your father working?"

"No."

"Is he at home?"

"He's dead," Julia says.

"I see."

Julia looks at the social worker. She says: "Could you find me somewhere to live in town?"

"Live here? Well . . . Shouldn't you be at school?"

No answer.

"Is there something wrong at home?"

Julia shakes her head.

"You want a job here?"

"Yes."

"Well, the first thing to do is to register for employment. You know where to go?"

"No."

"Next to the post office. You know where the post office is?"

"Yes," she lies.

"Well right next door. Meanwhile I'll write a letter to the Superintendent and ask what he thinks. Does your mother need you at home?"

"No," Julia says.

"Are you sure?"

"Yes."

"Where will you stay tonight, Julia?"

"I don't know."

"All right. Now you go down and register for employment and then come back later. We'll have to find you a place for the night and get in touch with your mother."

Julia sits very still for a moment and then walks out; she does not look back. The social worker writes a brief letter to the Indian Superintendent and looks through a list of boarding homes. None seems suitable.

Julia does not return to the office. How she passes the next five hours is not known. She is very tired. Someone has found her and given her a few drinks. She had made a quick friend and then run away. Long after dark she is picked up by the police and taken to the court room. She tries to climb out of the window but is caught and put in the corporal's office. She sits on a hard chair, her head on the desk, refusing to speak.

The social worker arrives.

"Julia. Why didn't you come back?"

No answer.

"Who gave you that bruise on your arm?"

"I don't know who they were. If I did I wouldn't tell."

"How did it happen?"

"I was trying to get away."

"You didn't want to stay with them? But you won't tell us who they were?"

"I just want to be left alone."

"Well. It's time you were in bed, anyway. Perhaps we can go and talk to your mother in the morning."

"I won't go home."

"Don't they treat you properly?"

"They drink all the time," Julia says.

"All right. Come on, now. I'm going to take you to a family who will look after you until tomorrow."

As they go out the corporal takes the social worker aside. "That's the girl who's supposed to be having a baby."

Julia is apprehended under the Protection of Children Act. She is taken before the magistrate to be identified. Her mother is in court.

Julia sits at the back of the court, her hands in her lap, her legs stretched out before her and her eyes hidden by long lashes. She does not appear to be interested in the proceedings.

The social worker outlines the circumstances leading up to the apprehension and then turns to the mother.

"You can identify Julia? Could you tell the court her date of birth?"

The mother is sullen. "We have done our best. She won't do anything I tell her. She should be sent away."

The magistrate asks: "It has been explained to you that Julia will remain in a foster home until the court hearing?"

"Yes."

"We'll set the date, then."

"I tried my best," the woman says.

"You do quite a bit of drinking at home?"

"No."

"Has Julia been at school?"

"We tried to make her go."

"All right. You come back at the end of the month. You will be informed of the date and the time."

"All right."

Julia is driven back to the foster home. For the moment, she is content. She visits the medical clinic. The snow is melting on the mountains and the warm, spring weather comes to the coast. She is learning how to live with white people. The foster father is curious; he asks questions about her home life and about the amount of alcohol consumed in her home and about love and hate and the village. Julia does not like the foster parents but, at first, she holds back her resentment. She spends a great deal of time in her room. She still likes to be left alone.

But as time passes she begins to lose her new identity. Each day passes without change, and for someone who likes to live in the present, this is not long endured. She helps in the house, eats her meals and does a little baby-sitting at night. She becomes a part of the scenery. Even the social worker seems to have forgotten her.

She realises that the foster parents have been kind to her. The day that she finds a twenty dollar bill in a drawer she decides to go home and she writes a polite letter to the foster mother and leaves it on the table. Then she walks down the hill to the main road and tries to stop a car.

Within half an hour the foster parents are out looking for Julia and they find her two miles down the road. She is trudging slowly through the dust, carrying her little blue suitcase.

She seems glad to be in the car. The foster parents drive to the social worker's office, and an interview takes place. Julia is tired, lethargic. The foster father is a little annoyed; he had expected gratitude. He cannot understand why the girl wants to go to a home that is of such a poor standard. The social worker is cautious.

She starts briskly. "You want to go home, Julia?"

The girl moves her head.

"You don't have to run away, you know. I thought you wanted to stay here until your baby was born."

"Why don't you come back with us?" the foster mother asks.

Julia remains silent.

Wearily, the social worker asks the foster parents to go home and wait; she sits behind the brown desk and looks at the face of the child. She reads the file again. There is a long silence. Julia sits very still. The woman and the girl are trying to understand one another.

"What don't you like about the foster home, Julia?"

"They're all right."

"But you don't want to stay there?"

"No."

"No special reason?"

"They ask questions all the time. And the kids don't do what I tell them. I do baby-sitting all the time. And washing dishes."

"Don't you do that at home?"

"Yes."

"I tell you what we'll do. You can go home for the week-end. By Monday I will have found a new foster home for you. Would you like that?"

Julia nods. She imagines the return home, the welcome and the admiration. She will show them all her new clothes and take some presents to her little brothers. And then she will leave again. Without realising it, Julia is beginning to look on her own village as a place of deprivation. Yet it still remains the source of her warmth and main influence in her thinking.

"All right," she says. "Could I collect my things first?"

"Of course."

They reach the village in the late evening. The social worker goes into the house. Julia's mother is standing in front of the sink. A man lies on one of the beds; he does not speak.

"I've brought Julia home for the week-end," the social worker says.

The mother does not look around. Julia walks into one of

the bedrooms and starts to unpack her case. The little boys watch her with excitement. Presently, the mother says:

"She's not staying here?"

"This is just a visit. Julia will have to return to a foster home on Monday."

The man props himself up on one elbow. "What about the family allowance?"

"Well?"

"We get nothing for her," he says.

"That's right."

He grunts and lies down again. The mother glances nervously at the presents Julia has brought for her brothers. After a while, the girl goes out to search for her friends.

"Have you discussed the baby?" the social worker asks.

The mother says: "I don't know. She can get it adopted if she wants. It's up to you."

"It's up to you and Julia."

"We'll talk about it," the man says. It is almost a dismissal. He turns over and looks at the wall.

The social worker leaves. On Monday, Julia arrives in town and is driven to her new foster home. By this time in her life she is more adept at judging adults, their children and their standards; she understands their thoughts and ambitions. She is able and willing to adjust in the interests of peace. And over the months, while she is waiting for the baby, she has long discussions with the social worker about the future, about adoption and about the completion of her education, a job, marriage and the whole contemplated pattern of her existence.

She is able to talk about such things with clarity, yet her mind and vision only grasp the present and the immediate future. She has not forgotten George and spends two weekends at home on the reserve.

Perhaps to gain sympathy, she tells the foster parents exciting stories of her home life. They, in their turn, become dedicated to the idea of saving the soul and body of the young girl whose personality they find mysterious and attractive. They become very critical of Julia's mother; they are angry with the social worker who plans to let Julia go home after the baby is adopted.

The day after Julia's baby is born, the girl asks to see the social worker and says that she has changed her mind. She wants to take the baby home. Her mother, her aunts and uncles, cousins and second cousins, all have been to see her or written to her. They all advise her to keep her baby. She complies, because she knows that her future is with her own people, and it will remain so until marriage between Indians and whites is more common and more accepted. She is discharged from hospital and vanishes into the obscurity of her own world.

The foster parents are angry, about Julia and about the baby. They ask if their name can be removed from the list of foster parents. The man says: "People like that should not be allowed to have children."

"Good morning, beautiful Julia. So you wish to be a nurse. Have you ever had TB?"

It is a year later. Julia is a character of contradictions, but she has acquired an identity. If nothing else, she is the mother of Sharon Amelia. She may not envisage a bright future, but at least she can accept plans that other people make for her.

Julia still has many loyalties, and if you should meet her in the city or if she is the nurse who tends you in hospital, do not praise her friends or criticise her enemies. The situation may be reversed tomorrow.

Her future is less definite. If she marries George and if he has a steady job and a good house, she will thrive and have the best of two worlds. But if George is more often than not unemployed and forced to live in a house with oil lamps and no water and a leaking roof, then the respite will be home brew on a Saturday night and, in five years, Julia will be unrecognisable.

# 16

# A Visit to Nuchatlitz

WE are half a mile off shore, flying between the grey winter clouds and the sea. I am delighted that we are on the way home. Only one thing remains to be done. We have to call in at the island village of Nuchatlitz and pick up a little girl who is returning to school. I read a magazine. The plane lurches in the wind. The pilot glances across to see if I have fastened my safety belt. He grins, quite happy to be on the west coast and not back in Newfoundland where he flew through frozen rain and was sometimes forced down between airfields. He has a road map on his knees.

The snow comes as we reach the mouth of Esperanza Inlet and turn away from the sea; it blows down from the mountains until we are in a shroud of white, cut off from the shore and the sky. Only the sea is visible, and we fly at a hundred feet above the waves. Nuchatlitz must be somewhere to the south, but it will be difficult to find. It is too late in the afternoon to be looking for a small island, and the snow drains daylight from the immediate sky. The pilot peers ahead, trying to pick out the shoreline, the dark shadow of trees or the lightness of a snow slope.

"We won't get home tonight."

"Where are you heading for?" I ask.

"Somewhere. Let's try Tahsis."

"Right."

The inlet is ahead. We cannot increase height and must follow the water, flying towards the east, to the narrows which will take us to a second inlet and to Tahsis. Even the small company town will be warm and cheerful after an hour in the snow-filled sky. And so we edge to the south. Once we have a shoreline to follow, we can make port. And in a sudden clarity between snow squalls we see the side of a mountain on our right, an indistinct shape of grey and white. We seem to be motionless in the air. Only the snow moves, streaking in from ahead and curving away behind us. The shoreline is under the right wing, and we turn to follow. Once, we are trapped in a bay, in a dead end with the mountains on two sides and the throttle is opened wide as we spin around. Try again. The tops of trees pass under the floats. We are back with the dark line of beach tracing a path for us below. In a little while there are lights ahead and we land in half darkness near the town. The pilot smiles.

"Let's go and have a drink."

We reach Nuchatlitz the following day. It is not the easiest place to find even in clear weather. Just one of nine little islands where the inlet reaches the Pacific. At low water it is connected by a sand bar with the next island. Many years ago, it was the village of great fishermen who made a habit of jumping from their boats on to the backs of whales. Each time the whale came to the surface they thrust in a spear, and each spear helped the men to reach the place behind the head from which they could kill with their harpoon.

There is not much activity in the village today. The church is not used. Five houses are occupied. There may be boats tied up at the dock. Possibly a cow at the edge of the trees behind the houses. The water in front of the village is like a lagoon, grey and shining as polished steel. The light, cool wind still blows from the mountains to the east, but the snow has melted. Blue smoke from the chimneys and dogs playing on the beach. As I walk up across the grass a young man who is drunk or angry or both stops me:

"What are you doing here? This is Indian land. Why don't you get off our land and leave us alone, white man?"

Why indeed? It is a question I sometimes ask myself. The children of Nuchatlitz live in their small island world and sometimes escape the educational nets set by the church or the government. Life is uncomplicated if you are not thinking about clocks and traffic and rent payments and air pollution. "Nuchatlitz" people will say. "Where is it? Who lives there? What do they do?"

In winter, the older people weave baskets which are decorated with a traditional pattern of whales and canoes. The old designs are handed down on a piece of jute sacking into which an astute ancestor wove pictures of the activities of her day. Strips of cedar bark and dried wild grass are used to make the baskets. Whenever I watch the weaving there are ten to fifteen loose ends being manipulated by the fingers of the weaver. The grass is worked around a block of wood which is later removed.

The young man walks away and the Chief Councillor comes towards me from the direction of his house. He is almost blind and walks with his head slightly averted. We shake hands in the centre of the beach. He looks physically strong, but cannot see well enough to work in one of the coast logging camps. But he often paddles off in his home-made boat, a hollowed-out log, several miles to an island where he cuts grass for the weavers. In a hot summer, when the village well runs dry, he brings water by boat from a small lake. He is a busy man. Apart from his duties as chief, he has a large family.

I ask: "What's Joe so angry about?"

"Joe? I don't know. He's like that sometimes."

"Often?"

"Sometimes he's like that. Quite often. Have you come to get Rosemary?"

"Yes."

"We expected you yesterday."

"It was the snow. We went into Tahsis for the night."

We walk up the beach to the house, which is comparatively new. Rosemary is seven, and will be going back to school after her Christmas holidays. She is one of my favourite children, and I have learned more from her than she has learned from me. Her first flight out was quite an adventure and her initial contact with foster home life was unfortunate.

213

I had placed her with a childless family about three weeks before school started. When I went back for a visit, the foster mother said: "Rosemary is a nice little girl but she never speaks." She had not said a single word, but had smiled, eaten her meals, slept well and looked at television. On the following day I moved Rosemary to a home where there was a girl of her own age. The two little girls started to play together and carried on long conversations which did not appear to be in Indian or English but in a language of their own. They could understand one another, which was the main thing.

A week later, Rosemary went off to school. Next morning I received a very cool telephone call from the school principal who asked if I thought he was running an institution for retarded children. Would I please come and collect the Indian girl at once.

I asked if he was referring to Rosemary, who was certainly not retarded but had learned to speak Indian as a child and came from an isolated island. I said that I was not an expert in educational affairs but had assumed that the first grade was for children who had not started to learn.

In the end, it did not seem worth arguing any more and Rosemary was transferred to a kindergarten. I asked various people to see her, supervisors and school psychologists, but none of them showed any desire to tackle the unknown. Rosemary remained in her kindergarten, where she proved to be intelligent and friendly. We discovered that she was a little deaf. Otherwise, she was a very normal child.

While Rosemary packs, I wander around the village and take photographs. It is cold on the beach. The open sea is dark grey, restless between storms. The mountains are not far to the east, and the trees above the three thousand foot level are covered with fresh snow.

I stop at the edge of the sea and look back towards the village. The island is flat, but one side is covered with trees. Where the houses stand, the grass is very short; it looks as if sheep have grazed there. A wooden figure, carved many years ago, stands between the houses and the beach. The Indians call it the Anchor Man and tell me that it warns them of the approach of strangers like myself.

Because of a decrease in population and an increase in such things as pensions and welfare payments, Nuchatlitz has achieved an economic soundness. The chief, whose name is Matthew, is unemployable and receives a monthly cheque from the Department of Indian Affairs. He is free to help the old people and the women who might otherwise have to move elsewhere. The younger men work for much of the year and can exist on their Unemployment Insurance between jobs because they pay no rent; no water rates, no electricity bills, no taxes, no telephone accounts. The education of the children is free. There is a small mission hospital ten miles up the inlet where babies are born and such things as broken arms and legs can be treated. The hospital is never so short of beds that people are discharged when there is a gale blowing and there is no way home across the sea. It stands on a low point of land under a mountain and was once a complex of services, medical, spiritual, educational and social. It is a small, Methodist beachhead in an otherwise Catholic area.

Matthew comes over to where I stand on the slope of the beach; he wants to discuss treatment for his eyes. And as we walk together around the curve of the shore we come to a place where a small, red plane is chocked up on wooden blocks. The propellor is bent. Matthew tells me that the pilot became lost, ran out of fuel and put the plane down on the sand bar when the tide happened to be out. It was very lucky. The plane was not seriously damaged, but the Indians have taken the wheels because they feel that the pilot made use of Indian land without permission. My first impulse is to tell Matthew that he has no right to remove the wheels of the plane which, in any case, landed below high water mark, outside the reserve. My second impulse is to mind my own business.

We return to the house. The room seems to be filled with children. Matthew's wife tells me that some of Rosemary's clothes have been washed but are not dry. Yes. They had a very good Christmas. She is quiet, practical, putting the final touches to the business of filling a suitcase and making parcels of the wet clothes. There is no need for me to leave the family alone for an emotional farewell. Rosemary accepts the fact of departure with equanimity, and her mother shows no sign of sadness. But in his own way, Matthew is making plans to visit the foster home. He thinks he might call in when he goes out to have the eye test. He has carved a totem pole for the foster parents and his sister is weaving a basket. He has great faith in people who try to help his small daughter. He has faith in the use of education. He will permit all the moves to take place and the plans to be implemented with certain reservations.

Matthew's faith in people who help his children will end if he senses that the motives are not correct or that there is something he cannot understand or that there is something he is not told. He will be angry if, for some reason, Rosemary does not arrive home on time for her holidays. It could be that someone is busy or lazy or indifferent. It might be that there is a simple misunderstanding. Matthew is very quick to judge the careerist or the researcher or the off-hand attitude of the pessimist. He cannot see very well and he is chief of a diminishing band on a small island, just about as far west as you can go without a boat. But he retains the right to be a husband and a father in his own way. The thread of trust between Matthew and myself is very frail. One day it will break. Sooner or later, a politician will change policy or an administrator will change practice or a foster parent will try to change Rosemary. In the twelve years it will take Rosemary to complete her education, something like that is bound to happen.

I am looking out of the window at the grass and the beach and the grey sea with clouds almost touching the trees on the next island to the north. There is something very poignant about the struggle of this little group of people whose happiness and sadness are so unrelated to mine, whose life has a style which is no longer significant. In the next house, the dyed grasses hang right across one wall and a woman spends her day weaving. In another house, a woman writes to her daughter, who is at school in a small mining town sixty miles to the east. When darkness falls and the oil lamps are lighted and the curtains drawn, the village will be nothing but a patch of darkness on the sea. It will probably snow during the night. And then, one day, summer will come. In how many years will the last person leave the village and the last boat head away up the inlet towards the east? It does not really matter very much except to people like Rosemary, who will have no refuge.

From the turbulent sky, we look down on the mists and the coast with the winter sea stretching away as far as the rain squalls. It is a scene of melancholy. When I turn to look at Rosemary, she smiles, showing no fear, and I remember that her grandfather had speared whales from a fifteen-foot boat.

## 17

# A Small and Charming World

As time goes by, all worlds change. I have tried, in this book, to show the moments of today which are more important than the ghost-ridden pages on anthropology or dismal prognoses on the future. It is easy to be angry. It is easy to hope that change will not come and that men in Indian communities will continue to show disdain for suffering, for want. Few of us remain outside the didactic optimism of the modern state. Few of us are free.

Perhaps this is sentimental. No one would wish a single child to die in childbirth or a single family to do without the comforts now available. I have no desire to destroy the truth of life in the Indian world. But anyone entering into that world will not be the same again. I was not there to teach but to learn. I was not there to condemn. The things I have omitted from these pages concern flaws in human nature, patterns of behaviour and those abnormal attitudes which are not uniquely Indian but derive from the very origins of man.

There were many short moments which created the hours of happiness and misery. I might have mentioned the snow falling on a small group of people as they walked to the graveyard, one man having a small coffin under his right arm. I can remember the day the young man drowned in the lake and we were unable to revive him. It was very hot, and we carried him down towards the village on a mattress. There must have been a hundred people there. The hearse arrived from town. It was a bright blue station wagon and the driver had brought his blonde girl friend along for the ride. The radio was playing and the girl was smoking a cigarette.

I might have written about the little hotel in Alert Bay where I used to pay a reduced rate for the room if the door had been smashed in the night before. And when we went down to the beer parlour there would be twenty people around a table. The barman used to revive those who were too drunk to walk by holding a bottle of ammonia under their noses. We used to take a taxi up to the reserve at midnight and talk through the hours until it was dawn. There was a winter evening when I stopped to see a doctor on the edge of a small community and found a naked man unconscious in the office and the doctor kneeling in the bedroom with a stethoscope held to the chest of his little dog. The man had poisoned himself and had vomited and the dog had come in to lick up the mess. The dog died and the doctor wept by himself in the bedroom while I answered his telephone.

There was a day when the X-ray technician arrived up

from the city and opened a crate she thought contained her equipment but found, instead, the body of an American sailor which was being taken down the strait for burial. I do not forget a young Indian girl who was described as a chronic delinquent by teachers and school counsellors and policemen and probation officers and judges and who was so angry at being arrested in the school classroom that she went on to become a graduate with top marks in Russian and Philosophy and English. There was a young man from a northern reserve who did not like the way I shrugged off his desire to be a bush pilot. He saved his money for two years and paid for all the hours to qualify for a commercial licence and then piloted one of the priests around the parish. There was another Indian pilot who flew to his death on a mountain while looking for a missing plane.

I could have written about the hours spent in the courtroom with the fly-specked picture of the Queen and the uncomfortable chairs and the young people who stood in the dock with their heads bowed so that their words were inaudible. I remember Madaleine, who did not speak a word in court for two hours and would not speak to me afterwards during lunch or during the long drive to her home. For five hours she was silent and for five hours she stared down at her lap as if the end of the world was at hand. I visited her home next day. The noise inside was deafening, and when I opened the door I saw Madaleine dancing on the table dressed in a scarlet coat, sea boots and black gloves. She was holding a wooden sword in her right hand. She turned to look at me and smiled with her seventeen-year-old eyes and bowed. I had caught her being herself.

You might have been interested in the spring day when people came from all over the north for the funeral and camped in the open spaces between the houses. There were a great many cars and trucks parked along the road and smoke was rising from the fires. It looked more like a fiesta than a funeral. Charlie told me that they could not close Mary's coffin until all her relatives had been made pure and that this had to be done before the priest arrived or the whole family would become sick. There were some things, he said, that doctors from the white town did not know about. Charlie looked so nervous that I opened the door of the car and we drove out to the house where Mary's husband and children were sitting. They all climbed into the back of the car and we returned to the village and as we went into the hall where the coffin lay there was a sudden silence outside as if three hundred people were holding their breaths. When we came out into the daylight the noise started again. The priest arrived ten minutes later.

There was a morning when I sat with a man and wife and listened to the fall rain against the windows. A dead baby lay in a coffin on the table. They had lighted candles at each end of the coffin and all morning people came in to pay their respects. The child looked as if it was asleep.

This book should have been about a world where little is sacred and where laughter is the best answer to confusion and small-mindedness and pomposity. I should have written about the many children who were lost and stranded and for whom I always found a home by knocking on a single door. I knew a man whose wife left him and, several years later, had a child and was found dead one day by a neighbour. When he heard about it the husband travelled three hundred miles to find and bring to his home the little girl who had been left without support. It was in this world of kindness and tranquillity that a young man returned from town and was asked by his mother not to drink so much. He promised he would not drink again and went into the bedroom where he kept his rifle and blew away the top half his skull.

The dark flaw in the human spirit is evident in all societies. And yet, while in Indian communities, I was not haunted by possibilities of disaster as I am in my own world. I did not feel the seed of self-destruction in the nature of our technical progress and social triumphs. We are not particularly safe behind a screen of missiles, but there is something comforting in the thought that, tonight, people sit before round metal stoves in their small houses on coastal islands while the gales blow and rain falls and the sea heaves against the shore. And in the morning the men will go out to see if the boats are safe and the women will start their endless washing and the children will run from house to house in the wind. The teacher will ring the school bell and the old women will weave the wild grasses. It will be an ordinary day.

# TOTEM BOOKS —

*What they are all about*

The importance of paper editions of strong best-selling hardbound titles in this country is growing. The Canadian reader requires a reliable source from which to collect a wide variety of Canadian writings.

Collins Publishers established their Totem Book division to bring top fiction, adventure, biographies and topical subjects to the bookshelf as well as the pocket in inexpensive editions. The books that everybody wants are in TOTEM.

Ask your bookseller about new releases.

*Colophon designed by Derek Carter*

The gentle bestseller that is sweeping the world

# I HEARD THE OWL
# CALL MY NAME

by
Margaret Craven
$1.25

Mark Brian, a young Anglican priest who has not long
to live, is sent to the Indian village of Kingcome in the
wilds of British Columbia.

While sharing the hunting and fishing, the festivals and
funerals, the joys and sorrows of a once proud tribe, Mark
learns enough of life to be ready to die.

"A beautifully told story."
*Vancouver Sun*

# A Totem Book

Footloose in Canada

# THE ANTE-ROOM

*Early Stages in a Literary Life*

## BY LOVAT DICKSON

Although his family was Canadian, Lovat Dickson was born in Australia and first saw Canada as a boy of fifteen. Almost at once he started to work. He wanted no more of school but to learn something of the vastness of the country.

In the next ten years he worked in many places including a mine in Ontario and a ship yard in Montreal. He put himself through the University of Alberta working as a chauffeur-guide in Jasper Park and as a free lance writer for the *Edmonton Journal*. After graduation he went to England and started his highly successful career as a book publisher (Among his authors was Grey Owl whom he discovered and whose friend he became).

But this book is concerned with his ten formative years in Canada. Written with candour and humour, and infused with a love for the country it makes for delightful reading.

*"An absolutely first rate book"* — *NEW YORKER*

$2.95

A Totem Book